FLORALCRAFTS

FLORALCRAFTS

50 Extraordinary Gifts and Projects, Step by Step

Gillian Souter
&
Catherine Lawrence

CROWN TRADE PAPERBACKS

New York

Published by Crown Trade Paperbacks, 201 East 50th Street, New York,
New York 10022. Member of the Crown Publishing Group.

Random House, Inc. New York, Toronto, London, Sydney, Auckland

CROWN TRADE PAPBERBACKS and colophon are trademarks of
Crown Publishers, Inc.

Originally published in Australia by Off the Shelf Publishing in 1995.

Manufactured in Hong Kong

LIBRARY OF CONGRESS CATALOGING-IN-PUBLICATION DATA

Souter, Gillian.
[Flower craft gifts and projects]
Floralcrafts: 50 extraordinary gifts and projects, step-by-step /
Gillian Souter & Catherine Lawrence.
          p. cm.
Originally published: Flower craft gifts and projects. Lewisham, NSW: Off
the Shelf Pub., 1995.
Includes index.
1. Flower arrangement. 2. Dried flower arrangement. 3. Nature craft.
I. Lawrence, Catherine. II. Title.
SB449.S583 1995
745.5—dc20   95-13003
                                              CIP
ISBN 0-517-88481-X

10 9 8 7 6 5 4

First American Edition

Foreword

Flowers have always been used to mark occasions of great significance, to bring pleasure to friends and family and to beautify the home both inside and out. If you've never tried much more than growing flowers or arranging them in vases, this book will start you on a journey of floral discovery and show you the many varied ways in which flowers can be used.

Here are the arts of drying and pressing flowers, of mixing them into fragrant potpourris and using their attributes to scent and flavor other things. There are even ideas for imitating flowers in fabric and paper. Each technique is described at the start of the chapter, followed by three imaginative projects which are identified by these motifs:

A personal item, ideal as a gift

Something useful for the home

Items for special occasions

There are also tips on wrapping flowers, on decorating boxes and baskets with them, and ideas for using them on gift tags and cards. One way or another, flowers make the perfect gift!

Contents

Flowers

Flowers have been cultivated for many thousands of years and, accordingly, are now amazingly diverse. Not only do they come in all colors of the spectrum, they also vary in shape and texture, in scent and longevity. You need not be a botanist to master the flower crafts in this book, but an appreciation of different types of flowers will take away some of the guesswork.

There is a flower for every shade of color imaginable. When selecting flowers, decide whether you want strong patches of solid color or variegated shades. Mixing colors in an arrangement is discussed on page 12. You must also choose from large flower heads, sprays of tiny blossoms, clumps of florets, or long stems with a series of flowers. Textures—waxy, glossy, serrated, creased, smooth—are also important. Some flowers, such as carnations and statice, last much longer than others like the short-lived violet and sweet pea.

These days, our choice of flowers is less dictated by the seasons than it was a generation or two ago. Flowers from other parts of the world are also commonly available. In some ways, both of these aspects lessen the natural impact flowers can have on us, but they also have obvious advantages.

The ideal source of flowers is your own garden. If you have any space to cultivate, you can have a constant supply of fresh flowers, many of which aren't grown commercially. The next best option is to visit your local flower markets where the flowers will be recently cut, the prices reasonable and the choice at its widest. If this is not feasible, hunt around for a good florist nearby.

Flowers used in the projects are all named, but note that others can often be substituted to achieve a similar effect.

Marigolds and lavender have qualities that are valuable in culinary and cosmetic preparations.

The cornflower is such a brilliant color that its name is often used to denote this shade of blue.

The short life of violets can be extended by crystallizing them with gum arabic and sugar.

Large blossoms dominate
a display and set the tone:
chrysanthemums suggest
a casual style, magnolias
sound a more formal note.

Roses are grown
in many colors,
shapes and scents
and have a
thousand uses
in flower crafts.

Bougainvillea
looks delightful
floating in a
shallow bowl.

Feathery sprays of
tiny flowers can help
to soften the outlines
of a display.

Foliage should
complement flowers
in an arrangement;
you may want to
select foliage from
a different plant.

The delicate nature of
some flowers makes
them of limited use
for arranging, but
these variegated
flowers would look
delightful pressed.

Equipment

The tools of a florist's trade are relatively minimal and readily available; most will already be found around the home. Those that aren't can be purchased from suppliers of craft materials or from large hardware stores.

Strong scissors or florist's snips are necessary for cutting thick stems and wires. Stub wires are used to wire individual flowers, bind arrangements and form the stems of many artificial flowers. They are available in various thicknesses and you must choose one suitable for the particular task. Stem tape is a worthwhile investment as it both binds and conceals any wires. Dry foam or oasis is an asset when arranging fresh or dry flowers and there are a range of guards and holders which make the task easier. A glue gun and a craft knife will be useful in many of the projects.

Specific techniques may require a few extra tools: these are explained in the introduction to each chapter. Equipment and materials needed for each project are listed in a box above the project picture. If you don't have a specified item, read the instructions and you may find that an alternative utensil will do the same job just as well.

Counterclockwise:
a craft knife; strong
florist's scissors; stub
wires & spool wire;
a block of dry foam;
stem tape.

1 It is a simple matter to make your own flower press. Cut two rectangles of sturdy ply. Tape them together and make a pencil mark in each corner. With a piece of scrap timber underneath, drill holes to match your bolt size.

2 Cut rectangles of blotting paper and cardboard the same size as your ply pieces. Use a ruler or a 45° triangle to cut off the corners. Assemble the press, with ply top and bottom and two sheets of blotting paper sandwiched between cardboard. Secure the bolts with wing nuts on top.

Clockwise:
a flower press;
a glue gun for fixing
dried flowers; a
meat tenderizer for
crushing stems;
a guard for securing
stems in dry foam.

Basic Techniques

Surprisingly few techniques need to be mastered before you can fully enjoy flower crafts. Most of them pertain to the preparation of fresh flowers to ensure that they last as long as possible, or to methods of drying flowers so that they last indefinitely. These are all discussed and illustrated over the following four pages.

Other techniques which apply to specific types of flower crafts, such as potpourri or pressed flower art, are discussed in the opening pages of their particular chapter.

One piece of advice is common to all flower crafts: handle flowers with care, as rough treatment can spoil their delicate qualities including appearance and taste.

Preparing Fresh Flowers

Pick flowers before the heat of the day or buy them before they reach the blowsy stage. Recut stems at a sharp angle and place them in water as quickly as possible. Different types of flowers need different treatments: woody stems need to be crushed, poppies and stems which exude a milky sap should be singed with a flame on the cut.

Soak flowers up to their necks in water for several hours before arranging them. If they are to be arranged in a container, remove any leaves which will be below the water line. Thorns can also be removed for easier handling. Replace the water in vases and containers daily, using fresh water at room temperature. Removing withered flower heads will encourage new buds to open.

Wiring is mainly necessary when fresh flowers need to be forced into a certain position, as in a garland or a bouquet. Instructions for wiring are given at the bottom of the next page.

◄ All stems need to be re-cut, even if they have just been picked. Cut them at a sharp angle, exposing a greater area for drawing water up the stem. Place them in tepid water as quickly as possible after cutting them.

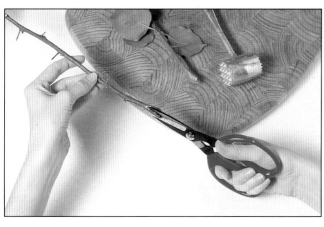

◄ Woody stems on flowers such as rhododendron, lilac and camellia need to be opened so that they can take up more water. First crush them with a hammer or meat tenderizer and then make a small split up the stem to allow water to be taken up.

► Strip off any foliage that will lie below the water line in an arrangement, as this will rot. For posies and other hand-held arrangements, break off thorns on the lower section of each stem.

► For hollow stems, such as delphinium and larkspur, simply insert a wire. For thin stems and sprays of fine foliage, twist a wire around the stalk. For large flower heads, pierce the calyx or base with a wire and twist the wire around the stem. If necessary, cover with stem tape to conceal the wire.

Drying Flowers

Flowers and foliage can be dried by various methods: some suit certain flowers more than others. The table below gives a rough guide to possible methods, but experimentation is the best way to find out what will work in your own specific conditions.

The simplest method for drying flowers is to let them dry out naturally, either by hanging them upside down in an airy room or cupboard or by standing them in a container which is empty or has very little water in it. Darkness helps to preserve the colors and it is important that bunches are well-spaced.

Flower heads can also be laid flat on a wire rack for drying. Those with a delicate struc-ture should be dried in a desiccant, such as silica gel crystals, alum, borax or fine sand. Clusters of flowers such as hydrangeas, or those with many tiny petals such as cornflow-ers, can be dried on paper towels in a micro-wave oven on a very low setting.

For all methods, the time required will vary depending on the amount of water stored in the flowers. Check regularly to see if petals are papery. Excessive drying in desiccant or in a microwave can make flowers very brittle. Once perfectly dry, they can be stored in boxes lined with tissue paper until required. Adding a few moth balls will lessen the chances of the flowers being eaten by insects.

POSSIBLE DRYING METHODS

Here are some choices for flowers which generally dry well:

❀   air drying - hanging
✳   air drying - upright
❖   desiccant
★   microwave

Achillea ✳ ❀	Geranium ❖	Narcissus ❖
Allium ❀ ✳	Golden rod ★ ❀ ✳	Pansy ❖
Agapanthus ✳	Grape hyacinth ✳	Peony ❖ ❀
Anemone ❖	Grasses ❀	Pink ❖
Buttercup ❖	Gypsophila ★ ❀	Poppy seed heads ❀
Camellia ❖	Heather ❀	Primrose ❖
Carnation ❖ ❀	Helichrysum ❀	Rhododendron ❖
Chamomile ❀	Hollyhock ❖	Rodanthe ❀
Chive flowers ❀	Hops ❀	Rosebuds ❀
Cornflower ★ ❀	Hyacinth ❖	Roses ❖ ❀
Daffodil ❖	Hydrangea ★ ✳	Safflower ❀
Dahlia ❖ ✳	Iris ❖	Sea lavender ❀
Delphinium ❀	Jasmine ❀	Sedum ★ ❀
Everlastings ❀	Laburnum ❖	Statice ❀
Fennel ❀	Larkspur ❀	Stock ❖
Feverfew ★ ❀	Lavender ❀	Sunray ❀
Gentian ❖	Lilac ❖	Sweet William ✳
	Lily ❖	Tansy ★ ❀
	Love-in-a-mist ❀	Violet ❖
	Marigold ❖ ❀	Yarrow ✳ ❀
	Mimosa ❀ ❖	Zinnia ❖

For hang drying, strip off unwanted leaves and bunch stems loosely so that flower heads are staggered in height. Secure the bunch with an elastic band, which will hold them in place as the stems shrink. Bend the two ends of a stub wire. Hook one under the band and use the other to hang the bunch.

Desiccant for drying flowers must be fine: crush silica gel crystals into smaller particles. Spread some desiccant in a box, rest the flower in it and gently sprinkle more desiccant into the flower head and between petals. Seal the box. Check regularly and remove flowers when dry. Dry the desiccant for re-use in a low oven.

Flower heads which have been dried in a desiccant may need to be wired before being added to an arrangement. Pierce the center of the flower with a stub wire, bend the end of the wire to form a small hook and pull it back into the flower head. Cover the wire stem with tape.

Many kinds of foliage can be preserved using glycerine. Half fill a container with glycerin and top it up with boiling water. Place the stems of foliage in the solution or submerge single leaves. Allow several weeks for absorption: leaves should remain glossy but may change color.

Fresh Arrangements

An "arrangement" sounds very formal, but it can simply be a single flower in a vase, half a dozen daffodils sprouting out of a teapot, or anything you choose to create. The main factors are the available flowers, the choice of containers, the setting for the display and, where relevant, the occasion.

We have looked briefly at selecting flowers on page 8. When combining different flowers you need to consider colors and scents. You might choose shades in the same sector of the color wheel or contrasting ones from opposite sides. Avoid mixing strong scents: combine fragrant flowers with less scented ones.

Containers aren't limited to vases; you can use anything that will hold water and can be made attractive. Baskets can be lined with plastic, terracotta pots can conceal a glass jar, decorator fabric can transform a plastic bucket. There are only a few considerations.

Flowers have a shorter life in shallow water. If the container is not very tall, or if it has no inwardly curving rim, the flowers may need support from a soaked oasis and wire mesh or a foam guard. Lastly, if you use a transparent container, the stalks become a part of the design. Keep the flowers and container in proportion: as a guide, the flowers should project to twice the height of the vase.

A floral composition is never viewed in isolation, but as part of a room. This doesn't mean you must slavishly match the curtains, but you should plan where the display will be placed and consider the larger effect as you work. The position will dictate whether it has a "front" or will be viewed from all angles. If it is to be displayed at a large gathering of people, make it grand enough to be noted.

Combining different flowers and maintaining a structure is a challenge. Try gathering flowers into a posy and then putting the whole thing in a vase. Alternatively, a block of foam gives you more control over the arrangement, as you can see in Project 3.

Marbles, pebbles or shells can all be used to anchor stems in a vase, and can add an aesthetic touch if the vase is transparent.

Color wheel
This wheel of primary and secondary colors is a useful way to consider the effects of combining colors. Complementary colors—those opposite one another—result in a bold contrast. Adjacent pairs create a more muted, harmonious effect. Pairs of alternate colors, such as blue and yellow, can be striking and eye-catching. The addition of white tends to boost other colors.

Extend the life of cut flowers by adding a few drops of bleach and a teaspoonful of sugar to the vase water.

PROJECT 1

Purple Haze

YOU WILL NEED
glass marbles
clear glass vase
strong scissors
long-stemmed flowers
foliage

Large arrangements can sometimes be quite top-heavy.
Adding marbles or shells to the vase will make the display
more stable while providing a decorative element.

1 ◄ Prepare the flowers by cutting the stems at an angle and splitting any woody stems (see page 13). Strip excess foliage off the lower stems. Our arrangement contains liatris (or gayfeather), various types of delphinium, rhododendron, Queen Anne's lace, sea lavender and variegated ivy.

2 ◄ Half fill the vase with water to give it some stability. Position those blooms with the largest stems in the vase. Here, the twisted rhododendron stems create a mesh to support other, more delicate stems.

3 ► Add marbles to the vase, dropping them in carefully around the main stems. Evenly space other large-stemmed blooms, such as the delphiniums and the liatris, wedging the stems in between the marbles.

4 ► Fill the gaps with floral sprays, such as Queen Anne's lace and sea lavender. Add several stems of contrasting foliage and some extra marbles if desired. Position the vase against a wall, as the arrangement is best viewed from the front.

PROJECT 2

Perfect Posy

"Posy" is derived from the same word as poetry: both are arrangements which convey a message. Wrapping the stems in damp tissues ensures the message will be fresh on arrival.

1 Choose flowers in several complementary colors: we have used red roses, yellow freesias, lavender and sea lavender. Strip off any foliage from the lower stems and remove any thorns or sharp pieces.

2 Take one of the larger blooms in one hand and add different flowers around it. The solid blooms form a gentle sphere, with finer sprays protruding. Turn the posy as you work and add each stem at an angle, as shown.

3 Secure the bunch of stems at the neck with an elastic band. Trim the stems so they are even and a comfortable length to hold. Cup several paper tissues around the stems, gather them in one hand and spray with water until quite damp.

4 Fold a cellophane sheet at an angle and wrap it around the posy. Repeat with another sheet. Form a bow from wired ribbon and thread an extra piece of ribbon through the back of it. Tie this tightly around the cellophane-wrapped stems and arrange the bow.

PROJECT 3

Easter Basket

YOU WILL NEED
a basket
plastic bowl or lining
an oasis
long-stemmed flowers
multi-blossom flowers
floral sprays

Here is a pretty display to celebrate Easter. Flowers with multiple blossoms on each stem give the arrangement the gentle appeal of a cottage garden.

1 *While you prepare the container, place the flowers in a bucket and fill it with water. Line a basket with plastic or fit with a plastic bowl. Cut oasis to fit and soak it in water for at least half an hour. Place the soaked oasis in the plastic bowl or lining. Secure it with a guard.*

2 *Sort the flowers: we have used blue and white delphiniums, "Cécile Brunner" roses, pink lupins, large yellow daisies and sprays of Queen Anne's lace, yarrow and feverfew. Cut each stem at a sharp angle and strip the foliage off the lower section. Create the basic structure with tall delphiniums.*

3 *Arrange other long-stemmed blooms, such as lupins, at different heights. Add flowers with multiple blossoms, such as clumps of roses and feverfew. If the display will be viewed from different angles, turn the basket as you work.*

4 *Add sprays of flowers, such as yarrow and Queen Anne's lace, in any obvious gaps. Put the arrangement in position and then fill up the container with water.*

Dried Displays

Not so very long ago the words "dried flowers" conjured up images of very dead, colorless flowers arranged in stark shapes. Now, with the inspiration of some very talented floral artists, the full potential of dried flowers is being realized. Formal displays of richly colored lavender and roses, frothy bunches of pastel blooms, rustic swags of wheat and raffia—all made with dried materials and none the less attractive for it.

The selection of flowers for drying is perhaps the most important factor in creating a beautiful dried display, as some blooms retain their shape and color better than others. A list of popular flowers for drying appears on page 14, along with instructions for drying them. When buying ready-dried flowers, make sure the blossoms are undamaged and do not smell dank or musty.

A well-constructed dried flower arrangement will last far longer than a fresh one and so it is worthwhile spending more time and effort on its composition. As no water is required, you have greater freedom. You can select unusual containers that are not watertight or can create uncontained structures such as stacks, garlands, swags or frames. Dry foam can be used to support stems and so create more elaborate displays. Flower heads can also be glued in place with a hot-glue gun.

The fragrance of flowers tends to fade during drying, but can be refreshed in several ways. Loose potpourri can be sprinkled into the container of an arrangement or sachets of it tucked in amongst the stems. Alternatively, a few drops of a suitable essential oil can be used, but be careful not to dampen the flower heads or they may rot.

Although a dried arrangement lasts indefinitely, it still needs some attention. Remove any dust with a hair dryer on a cool setting. Do not place the display in direct sunlight or the colors will fade. If they do, replace those most affected with newly dried flowers.

Statice and helichrysum are among the easiest flowers to dry effectively.

Most flowers dry best if picked just before they blossom. Hydrangeas are an exception; leave them on the plant until they start to lose color.

To make a bouquet in a basket, fix a small block of dry foam in the center. Insert long-stemmed flowers such as delphiniums at one end. Push larger blooms such as helichrysum, statice and roses into the top of the foam. Add sprays of sea lavender to soften the shape. Insert pieces of stem at an angle at the base. Wire a bow and insert it so that it covers the area where the stems enter the foam.

This flat arrangement of roses, pearl yarrow and moss is more formal. The tightly-packed flower heads have been pushed into a bed of dry foam.

PROJECT 4

Potted Garden

YOU WILL NEED
a terracotta pot
a foam block
stems of grain
long stemmed flowers
roses
a kitchen knife
secateurs
strong glue
ribbon

This bright no-maintenance garden will bloom all the year-round. When selecting the flowers, choose contrasting colors to make the display all the more striking.

1 Dry the flowers (see pages 14-15) or select suitable dried flowers. Use a long knife to trim the foam block to fit your terracotta pot: it should sit 1 " below the rim. Apply glue to the base of the foam block and insert it in the pot.

2 Cut the stems of the grass heads so they are an even length (we have used barley). Insert a row of them into the foam block at the back of the pot. Add two more rows, staggering the stems so that the gaps are filled.

3 Add several rows of flowers (we have used purple statice, Mexican daisies, lavender and roses). The arrangement should appear full but formal. Add some dried leaves at the front edges of the arrangement.

4 Cover any visible areas of the foam block with leaves, petals or small flower heads. Use wired or paper ribbon to tie a full bow and glue it onto the front of the pot.

PROJECT 5

Country Stack

YOU WILL NEED
raffia
strong scissors
stub wires
foliage
grasses
cones
flowers

This stack makes the perfect floral gift as it stands alone and doesn't require any special container. A raffia bow completes the look, or substitute paper ribbon in a complementary color.

1 ▶ *Dry a range of leaves, flowers and grasses or buy dried materials and strip excess foliage off the stems. Our example includes wheat, eucalyptus leaves, teasels, banksia, sea lavender, white helichrysum and cedar cones. The cones and any flower heads with delicate stems should be wired individually; see page 15.*

2 ▶ *Set the wired helichrysum aside. Start a bunch with several of the other stems and add to it while holding the bunch tightly in one hand. Continue to add stems at an angle, lowering the heads slightly as you work outwards. Bind the stack tightly at the stems with stub wire or string.*

3 ▲ *Poke the helichrysum (or other wired flowers) into the stack to fill any gaps.*

4 ▲ *Cut strands of raffia and loop them to form a large bow. Bind the loops of the bow with another length of raffia and then tie the ends around the stack, concealing the wire. Trim the knot ends at the back of the stack.*

5 ▶ *Check that the stack stands without support. If necessary, trim any stalks which prevent it from doing so.*

PROJECT 6

Welcome Vase

A petal-filled vase of dried flowers can be made when the baby is due and will transform the baby's room into a welcoming place for both mother and child.

YOU WILL NEED
clear glass vase
dry foam ball
double-sided tape
a glue gun
stub wires
ribbon
flower petals
dried flowers
dark leaves

1 Collect flower petals and dry them loose on a tray in a warm dark place. Hang-dry complete flowers and wire any delicate stems. Fill a vase with the dry petals or, if you do not have enough, place a ball of newspaper in the vase and surround it with petals.

2 If necessary, trim the foam ball so that it will sit firmly on the neck of your vase. Line the rim of the vase with double-sided tape and secure the foam ball on top.

3 Fix the dried flowers securely into the ball, starting at the top and working down and around. We have used roses, white helichrysum and sea lavender. Include dark dried leaves, such as beech leaves, for contrast.

4 Use a glue gun to attach the last blooms, filling any obvious gaps. Make a ribbon bow by forming two loops and binding the center with a wire. Stick the wired bow into the foam ball.

Miniatures

Arrangements of flowers need not always be on a grand scale and this chapter looks at some of the occasions when smaller is better. Creating miniature floral displays is also a good way of learning the basic techniques developed elsewhere in this book. The projects which follow give you practice in wiring fresh flowers, working with a wreath base and creating a topiary ball.

Small projects need fewer flowers and so are less likely to need a trip to the market or to the florist. Even if your garden is a tiny one, there are probably enough flowers to create modest displays, which are ideal when space is confined. A desk top, windowsill or bookshelf are all made much more cheerful by the addition of a few flowers. Arrange them in small containers: tiny pots or baskets, a milk jug, an egg cup, or even a pretty cup and saucer.

Use small flower heads, such as rosebuds, sweet william and pinks, or a few sprays from a stem of sea lavender or gypsophila. If you are using dried flowers, you can use the florets off a large flowerhead such as hydrangeas. Odd offcuts of dry foam will help secure arrangements in containers. A thin stub wire concealed with a narrow ribbon will be sufficient to bind a miniature posy.

Such mini bouquets make delightful decorative touches on gift tags, presents or napkin rings, and a fragrant one on a guest's pillow or linen makes a warm welcome. If you have enough flowers to make several mini bouquets, they will make colorful decorations on a Christmas tree. Small flowers are also ideal for children to wear and as well as making tiny posies, you can decorate hairbands for flower girls at a wedding.

Some craft stores stock miniature ceramic semi-circular pots which will lie flat against a wall. A series of these filled with cottage garden flowers make a pretty display. More formal arrangements—red rosebuds ringing a clump of lavender—can be very striking.

Tiny bouquets
These two posies are examples of dried and fresh flower bouquets in miniature. The first contains statice, pink sunrays, and sea lavender. The other, which includes small cornflowers, lavender and heather, is kept refreshed by a supply of water in the cellophane wrapping.

Potted miniatures
A small piece of dry foam keeps these dried flowers in place. Included here are yarrow, sunrays, morrison and a brown grass.

PROJECT 7

Candle Rings

YOU WILL NEED
small wicker rings
candles (see p.86)
small flowers
dried moss
scissors
a glue gun
a knife & mat

Decorate plain wicker rings with your favorite flowers and the result is simple elegance. Tea roses and white candles create a romantic ambience for that special night at home.

1 ▶ *Make plain candles to fit the wicker rings (see pages 86-87), or buy them ready-made. They must be quite tall so that the candle flame is not near the floral decoration.*

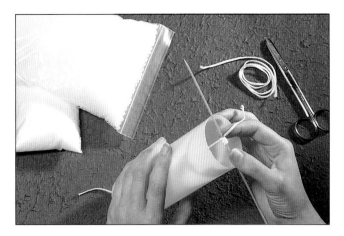

2 ◀ *Dry the flowers as instructed on pages 14-15. We have used small rosebuds and hydrangeas. Cut the flower heads from the stems with a pair of scissors.*

3 ◀ *Using a glue gun, dab a small amount of glue around a wicker ring and apply some moss. Apply glue to the back of each rose and glue in place, alternating the colors if you have two shades of roses.*

4 ▶ *As an alternative, glue bright red roses onto a wicker ring and fill the gaps with hydrangea flowers. Fit the candles in the rings. NOTE: Do not leave the candles burning unattended as dried flowers are highly flammable.*

PROJECT 8

Floral Sprays

YOU WILL NEED
flowers
foliage
stub wires
stem tape
strong scissors
narrow ribbon

Corsages and boutonniere are often worn at weddings but any event worth celebrating offers an excuse to decorate yourself with flowers.

1 | *Select suitable flowers: you will need several feature blooms and some finer sprays. We have used hothouse roses, a chrysanthemum, lavender, gypsophila and sea lavender. Wire the large blooms separately and the finer ones into small sprays (see page 13) and tape the top of each stem.*

2 | *Wire stems of foliage separately. Included here are ivy and leaves from jasmine and spider plants.*

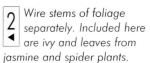

3 | *To make a boutonniere, combine one feature bloom with several leaves, bind with wire and stem tape. To make a corsage, bind the sprays of fine flowers to several stems of foliage with a stub wire.*

4 | *Add the feature blooms and bind with another stub wire. Form a bow from narrow ribbon and bind it with a wire. Add this to the corsage and wrap stem tape around all the wires. Refrigerate until required and then spray lightly with water. The corsage is worn with the flowers pointing downwards.*

PROJECT 9

Topiary Tree

For those who don't favor lavish floral arrangements, a miniature tree makes an interesting feature on a desk or mantelpiece.

YOU WILL NEED
a pot
a foam ball
a thick stick
plaster of paris
padding wrap
dried moss
stub wires
dried hydrangeas
glue
paper ribbon

1 *Cut a stick to about three times the height of your pot. Pierce the foam ball with the stick. Line the pot with plastic padded wrap or foam and fill it with plaster of paris. Stand the stick straight in the pot and support it with spare sticks. When the plaster has set, remove the padding.*

2 *Fix the foam ball on the stick so that it is pierced half way. Cut short sections of wire and bend them in half to form staples. Cover the ball with handfuls of moss, using the staples to pin it in place.*

3 *Snip florets of dried hydrangeas or other small flowers close to the calyx. Glue individual flowers onto the moss. Turn the pot and continue gluing until the ball is evenly covered.*

4 *Cover the base of the tree with dried moss to conceal the plaster. Cut a length of paper ribbon and glue it around the pot. Make decorative crosses from small pieces of ribbon and glue them in place.*

Balls & Swags

Floral displays come in all shapes and sizes. Spheres of flowers are particularly attractive and have many uses. Small scented balls or pomanders will perfume a room. Flower-studded balls can be hung as decorations or stuck on stems to form topiary trees. Brides and flower girls might carry beribboned flower balls instead of bouquets. A ball in festive greens and reds can be hung at Christmas as a replacement for the mistletoe.

Ready-shaped balls of dry foam or polystyrene are available in various sizes. You can, however, make your own by wrapping wire mesh around offcuts of dry foam and padding it with moss. Covering a ball requires a large amount of floral material. One option is to use a bulky and inexpensive material as a background and then add feature blooms.

Swags, long strands decorated with fresh or dried flowers, are perfect for hanging along a bannister, above a fireplace or over a doorway, or simply for laying on a tabletop. They can be formed either by adding floral material to a solid base, such as a raffia plait, or by wiring bunches of flowers and foliage along a length of rope so that each one overlaps the last. Projects 11 and 12 are examples of each of these methods.

Ribbons, cones, berries and fruit can all be wired and included in a swag for extra interest. Dried orange slices or whole apples make particularly colorful additions.

Whether you are working on a swag or a sphere, delicate flowers and sprays will need to be wired before being used. Refer to page 13 for instructions on wiring. It is best to gather all materials and plan the arrangement of them first. Check whether you have enough of everything, then wire and trim them to size before assembling the project.

1 *Floral pomanders make a pretty decoration as well as a sweet-smelling means of deterring insects. (For a hanging loop, push two ends of a bent stub wire through the ball and bend the ends to secure.) Apply glue to a small section of a dry foam or polystyrene ball and roll it in loose lavender. Continue until the ball is covered.*

2 *Apply glue to the back of a dried flower and stick it on the pomander ball. Continue adding flowers one at a time until you are satisfied with the result.*

Wire-edged or twisted paper ribbons are a swag-maker's delight as they will hold their shape well.

Cones make an attractive addition to a swag. Wire pine cones around the base so they can be easily attached.

PROJECT 10

Rosebud Ball

YOU WILL NEED
stub wires
a foam ball
dried rosebuds
glue
ribbon
rose oil

This simple but eye-catching rosebud ball makes a thoughtful and attractive gift. A smaller version would also make a lovely decoration for a flower girl to carry.

1 Bend a stub wire in half and push the two ends right through the foam ball to form a hanging loop. Bend each end over where it emerges at the other side to secure the wire. Thread a ribbon through the wire loop and tie a bow, leaving long ties for hanging the ball.

2 Sort dried rosebuds into small, medium and large. Apply a line of glue around the middle of the foam ball and attach a row of medium rosebuds. If the buds have any stem, pierce the foam ball with the stem, so that the bud is firmly fixed in place.

3 Add another line of glue to divide the ball into quarters and fix medium-sized rosebuds in place. Fill in each quarter with more buds, making sure that size changes are gradual.

4 Add a few drops of rose oil to the completed ball. Tie the long ends of the ribbon at the appropriate length. Hang the ball in a cupboard or from a shelf bracket. Refresh the scent when necessary with extra rose oil.

PROJECT 11

Raffia Plait

Enhance a dressing table or a kitchen wall with a pretty swag made from dried flowers and raffia. This simple project requires very little time and only a few materials.

YOU WILL NEED
raffia
stub wires
strong scissors
a glue gun
organza ribbon
bleached leaves
dried flowers
grasses
wheat
cones

1 Gather raffia to the desired thickness. Bind it at one end with a wire and secure it tightly. Divide the raffia into three equal parts and plait it by winding the left and then right strand into the center. If you want a curved swag, pull tighter on one side as you plait. Bind the end with wire and trim neatly.

2 Glue pale or bleached leaves in place. Wire small bundles of brown grass, quaking grass and wheat. Fix these onto the swag with a glue gun, arranging them so that they fan out from the center.

3 Apply glue to the back of cones and attach them to the swag. Glue on the dried flowers, such as roses, leucospermum and helichrysum, concealing any wires and filling any obvious gaps.

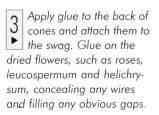

4 Make bows from wide organza ribbon by forming two loops and binding the center with a stub wire. Decorate each end of the swag with a ribbon bow.

PROJECT 12

Fireplace Swag

This Christmas swag could easily be adapted for harvest festivals by using fruit and wheat sheaves. It would also look wonderful over a door or window, or as a feature on a wall.

YOU WILL NEED

rope
stub wires
strong scissors
foliage
wide ribbons
artificial cherries
artificial berries
cones
gold spray paint
tape or hooks

1 ► Cut a length of rope so that it hangs under your mantelpiece and the ends fall halfway to the floor. Twist stub wires around it in three places and attach these to the underside of the mantelpiece from hooks or with heavy duty tape. Bind stems of foliage with stub wires; we have used camellia leaves and holly.

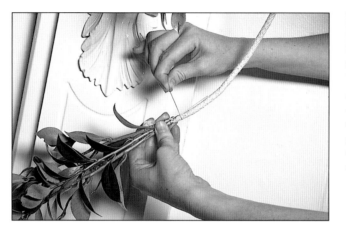

2 ◄ Start at the center and bind the foliage onto the rope with stub wires so that the foliage points inwards. When you reach one of the hanging points, stop and return to the center, then work outwards to the other hanging point. Finally, wire foliage to each end, starting from the bottom and working up.

3 ◄ Make bows by forming two loops in wide ribbon and securing the center with a wire. Spray artificial berries gold and attach some to the center of tartan bows. Spray some leaves gold and wire them in small sprays. Wire pine cones by looping a wire around the base and twisting the ends together.

4 ◄ Wire a large bow to each hanging point, and the smaller ones at intervals along the swag. Wire on the cherries, cones and gold leaves evenly, leaving the ends of the swag undecorated. Ensure that all wires and sections of rope are concealed and that the swag appears balanced.

Floral Frames

Frames provide a wonderful, but often overlooked, opportunity to decorate with flowers. Mirrors, which may otherwise appear blank, can be made into a feature by the addition of a lavish floral arrangement. Cherished photographs can also be given more prominence with a simple surround of buds or petals. A marriage certificate can be lovingly decorated with dried or pressed flowers from the bride's bouquet. A child's drawing can be awarded a chain of bright flowers as a border.

You do not need any existing frame base to work on: you can glue flowers directly onto the edges of an unframed mirror or picture. This will, however, be permanent as the glue can only be removed with difficulty. It is easier to add flowers to a base and, indeed, flowers are a good way to give an old or damaged frame a second life.

When you plan your project, decide whether or not the frame will be visible beneath the flowers and foliage. If the frame is worn or chipped, give it a coating of spray paint or conceal it fully with leaves, grasses or sprays of small flowers.

Small frames can be made from card of a suitable color, or from board covered with a fabric which complements your choice of flowers. Natural colors usually work best with dried flowers.

Choose flowers that have kept their color and shape well during the drying process: ones that have faded a great deal will tend to make the design look tired. The size of the frame should also affect your choice as large flowers will not suit a small frame. For such frames, you might use buds or petals, as we have done in Project 14. The design needn't be perfectly balanced—consider using a feature bloom or other large item, such as an attractive shell, in one corner and smaller flowers or simply foliage or moss around the rest of the frame.

A glue gun is extremely handy when you wish to fix dried flowers permanently in position. The easiest type to use are those with a trigger.

A floral decoration needn't cover the frame completely. Here, dried roses add a touch of nostalgia without hiding the elegant shape of the frame.

If framing a picture, be careful not to overwhelm the image with the various flowers surrounding it, either in terms of size or color.

A simple design of rosebuds makes a pretty frame for a photograph. Slice them in half so that they sit neatly on the card.

Green, white and gold are an excellent color combination. These dried sunray flowers are glued on with ivy leaves which have been preserved in glycerin.

PROJECT 13

Spring Border

YOU WILL NEED
a mirror & frame
a glue gun
strong scissors
stub wires
fine floral sprays
spring flowers

The frame of a dressing-table mirror comes to life with this lasting arrangement of brightly colored flowers. Vary the shades and types of flowers to complement your existing decor.

1 ▶ Dry a collection of bright flowers, such as delphiniums, white daisies, pink everlastings, statice, as well as some sprays such as sea lavender, gypsophila and clumps of hydrangeas. See pages 14-15 for instructions.

2 ▶ Cut small sprays of sea lavender and bind them with stub wires, then do the same with the statice. You will need approximately twice as many bundles of the sea lavender as of the statice.

3 ◀ Using a glue gun, apply a patch of glue to an old frame and stick down a wired bundle of sea lavender. Overlap the next bunch slightly and repeat this around the frame. Next, glue down wired statice at regular intervals. Make sure the outside of the frame is adequately concealed.

4 ▶ Cut the remaining flowers from their stems and apply glue to the back of the flowers. Glue them onto the frame, filling any gaps and covering all the wires. Fit a mirror in the recess of the frame.

Suggestion: If the frame will stand on a shelf or table, glue fewer flowers at the base.

PROJECT 14

Petal Frame

In this project, the jewel-like colors of dried petals are set off by a black lacquer base and a hint of gold. The result is a splendid surround for a special photograph.

YOU WILL NEED
thick black card
a black felt pen
a gold pen
tracing paper
a pencil & ruler
a knife & mat
a brush
acrylic varnish
glue
dried flowers

1 ▶ Measure the dimensions of your photograph. Cut a piece of black card with a window slightly smaller than the photograph and a border 2.5 " wide. Cut a back section the same size. Trace the pattern for the stand onto card: do not cut along the dashed lines. Color the rim of all pieces with the thick black felt pen.

2 ▲ On the front section, rule gold lines around the edges and window to form a grid as shown. When the gold lines are dry, apply a coat of acrylic varnish.

3 ▶ Working in one grid block at a time, spread a layer of glue with your finger. Sprinkle small dried petals onto the area; we have used lavender, rose, and marigold petals. When the glue has dried, shake off the excess petals and then glue extra petals to fill the gaps. Repeat for each block.

4 ▶ Run a knife lightly along the dashed lines of the stand and ease it into shape. Glue the stand onto the backing section to suit the orientation of your photograph. Stick the photograph on the other side of the backing section and glue the decorated section on top.

PROJECT 15

Hallway Mirror

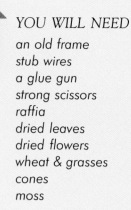

The warm natural shades of this frame capture the harvest mood. Hang it near your favorite raffia hat and let a bit of the country into your home.

1 Collect floral material: we have used eucalyptus leaves, various grasses, cedar and protea cones, banksia pods, teasels, yellow roses, white helichrysum and Spanish moss. Use a glue gun to cover an old frame with dried leaves. Dab glue directly onto the frame and then stick each leaf in place.

2 Plait a length of raffia for decoration and bind the ends with wire (see page 45 for how to plait). Glue the ends onto the top of the frame so it will arc over the mirror.

3 Cut ears of wheat and short stems of quaking grass or similar and bind them with stub wires.

4 Start at the base of the frame and glue the bundles of wheat and grasses at intervals along one side. These should point towards the top. Return to the base and repeat with the other side. Glue down small clumps of moss, and add cones and teasels in groups of two or three.

5 Cut the flowers from their stems and apply glue to the back of the flowers. Glue them onto the frame in generous clusters, filling any gaps and covering all the wires. Fit a mirror in the recess of the frame.

Table Arrangements

The dining table is one place where all the senses can be fully indulged. The taste of good food, the feel of linen napkins, the sound of pleasant conversation, are all enhanced by the sight and smell of flowers. Whether they are simply strewn over the tablecloth or arranged in an elaborate composition, they can turn a shared repast into a special event.

Choose flowers in colors that will complement your table linen and dinner service, and also to fit the occasion. A silver, ruby, or golden wedding anniversary dinner calls for special attention to color. Wedding arrangements should complement the color of the bridal party's clothing. If you are dining outside, flowers of the season are particularly fitting. When planning an evening meal, remember that very subtle shades may lose their effect in dimmed lighting.

Think about how the table will be viewed. At a dinner table, it is important that an arrangement is low and does not block people's view or make conversation difficult. If the table will be viewed from a distance, as would the bridal

table at a wedding or a buffet table at a banquet, consider decorating the sides with garlands of fresh flowers. For a low serving table, you might create a garland of flowers or place a bouquet with flowers facing out.

If there is limited space on the table, as there often is, try combining decoration and function. Some ideas—a napkin ring and condiments basket—appear in this chapter. If there is absolutely no space on the table, you might decorate the back of each chair with a swag, offering a warm invitation to guests and a gift for them to take home.

Consider other decorative elements on the table and make sure they don't compete. Candles can, for instance, be incorporated into a floral centerpiece (as in the simple designs in Project 7) or the two can be combined in a floating display. The plates themselves can be garnished with some of the edible flowers listed on page 145. When adding such details, make sure that the overall effect is pleasing to the eye.

A ring of flowers around each dinner plate is an attractive way to decorate the table when space is tight. Choose flowers that will last the duration of the meal, give them a long deep drink, and arrange them loosely just before the meal begins.

A bowl of floating flowers and candles adds a beautiful touch to the table. Candles with rounded bases float best.

PROJECT 16

Napkin Rings

Once made, these classic napkin rings can be used over and over again by replacing the flower spray afresh each time.

YOU WILL NEED
a cardboard tube
wire-edged ribbon
a sharp knife
a needle & thread
strong scissors
stub wires
stem tape
flowers
foliage

1 ▶ *Select a wide ribbon that has wired edges. Cut a section of cardboard tube slightly narrower than the ribbon. Cut two lengths of ribbon: one for inside the cardboard ring and the other for the outside. Stitch the ribbon edges together, so the cardboard ring is enclosed.*

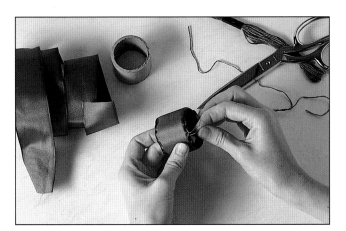

2 ◀ *Cut another length of ribbon and tie it to form a lavish bow. Stitch the bow onto the covered ring at a jaunty angle.*

3 ◀ *Cut large flowers and stems of complementary foliage: we have used canna lilies and a spray of nandina foliage. Wire each stem separately (see page 13 for detailed instructions).*

4 ▶ *Bind the wired flowers and foliage together with stem tape and bend the stem to form a hook. Place the napkin in the ring and hook the floral spray into the ring. Arrange the bow.*

PROJECT 17

Centerpiece

YOU WILL NEED
a shallow bowl
an oasis
large blooms
foliage
strong scissors
wire

This dramatic table arrangement boasts striking red parrot tulips, as well as irises, speciosum lilies and red fuchsias. A display such as this will brighten any occasion.

1 ▶ Cut the stems of the flowers at an angle and leave them in a bucket of water for several hours before arranging them. Cut an oasis to fit the bowl and soak it in water for an hour. Secure it in the bowl with wire.

2 ◀ Insert stems of foliage into the oasis so that the edges of the bowl are well concealed. We have used fuchsia stems with plenty of leaves.

3 ▶ Position the largest blooms (here, the lilies) in the center. Cut the tulip stems at different lengths and place short ones around the lilies. Position some long stems at either side, forming a diamond shape.

4 ▶ Add blooms in a contrasting color (here, the iris). Place the arrangement on the table and top up the bowl with water.

PROJECT 18

Vinegar Basket

Bottles and jars of condiments can be arranged in a pretty basket before being carried to the table. Choose a napkin and ribbons to complement the dried flowers.

1 Select dried flowers which will complement each other: we have used blue delphiniums and pearl yarrow. Bind sprays of small flower heads with stub wires.

2 Tie bundles of cinnamon sticks tightly with ribbon. Cut ears of wheat leaving just a small section of stem. Gently snip the flowers off delphinium stems (or other flowers).

3 Use a glue gun to attach ears of wheat around the rim of the basket. Next, glue a wired spray of the small flowers between each ear of wheat. For both of these, dab the glue onto the basket and then put the material in place.

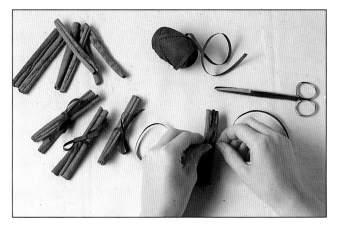

4 Dab glue onto bundles of cinnamon and stick them at intervals around the rim. Finally, dab glue onto the delphinium flowers and arrange them around the rim, being careful to fill any gaps and cover visible wires.

Wreaths & Garlands

Rings or circles have always carried a strong symbolism for all cultures, suggesting as they do the cycle of the seasons and even that of life and death. The ancient Greeks and Romans awarded wreaths of leaves as a mark of honor and glory. Flowers have long been twisted into garlands for brides and bridegrooms. Sheaves of wheat and corn were commonly woven into circlets at harvest time and the practice of hanging a welcoming wreath on the door of the home is an old and widespread tradition.

Garlands and wreaths can be made just by binding a bunch of floral material onto another, then adding a third and so on, but it is easier to add material to an existing base. Bases can be made from twined vines, cane, straw, wire, or any length of material that can be shaped and secured. A range of bases is available commercially, including polystyrene ones, but it is rewarding to make your own.

The type of base you select will be determined by various things such as how the garland will be hung or worn, the occasion or season, and the materials you have for decorating it.

If the wreath base is made of non-natural material, such as wire, foam or polystyrene, you will need to conceal it fully with stem tape, moss or leaves. Usually, foliage or grasses are attached to the base first to form a background. Delicate flowers may need to be wired before they are added, as will clusters of flowers with small heads (see page 13 for more details on wiring). These and other materials can be secured on the base using a binding wire, staples or a glue gun, depending on the type of base.

Add material evenly around the base to ensure a balance of color and weight. Moss or extra flowers can be added last to fill any unsightly gaps.

Garlands can be decorated with fresh or dried flowers to suit the occasion. Experiment when drying to see which flowers retain colors and shapes well.

Moss has been wound around this wire base and then secured with a piece of twine.

Staples of bent stub wire are useful for pinning leaves onto a foam or polystyrene base. Be careful to cover the staples with floral material.

PROJECT 19

Head Circlet

YOU WILL NEED
white roses
camellia leaves
fine-leaf creeper
stub wires
stem tape
strong scissors

This enchanting circle of white roses is guaranteed to make the wearer feel special. For a sturdier arrangement, wire the roses individually before binding them into the circlet.

1 *Place the roses in a bucket of water and let them drink deeply for several hours. Join two stub wires by twisting one around the end of the other. Cover this long wire with stem tape. Form a loop in one end and secure it by twisting the wire back on itself.*

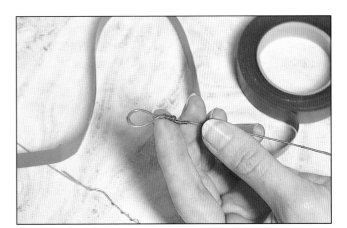

2 *Cut sprigs of leaves and strands of creeper. Cut roses leaving only a short stem. Lay a sprig of leaves along the covered wire and bind the stem on with a taped stub wire. Angle a rose away from the leaves but parallel with the bound stem and continue winding the stub wire so that it binds the stem of the rose.*

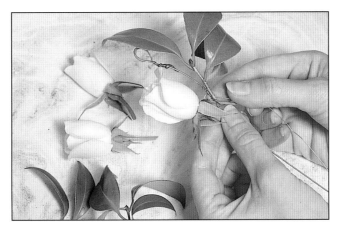

3 *Bind two or three roses in a row and then add a sprig of leaves and a strand of creeper. Repeat the sequence, taking up a new stub wire when necessary. Work along the taped wire, testing the circlet for size after a while.*

4 *Finish by binding a rose in the opposite direction so that its stem is concealed by foliage. Thread the taped wire through the loop, turn it and twist it back on itself, then tape the double wire. Store in a plastic bag in the refrigerator until required.*

PROJECT 20

Valentine Garland

Hearts and roses each speak the language of lovers. When combined in such an eloquent manner their message is clear and sweet. Delight someone you love with this exquisite garland.

YOU WILL NEED
roses
hydrangeas
dried moss
a clothes hanger
wire cutters
jute or string
a glue gun
strong scissors

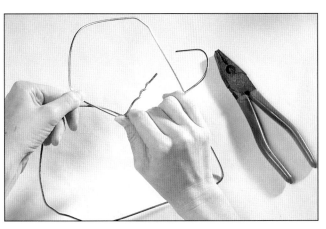

1 ▲ *Select roses with half opened flower heads in pastel shades. Dry the hydrangeas and roses as instructed on pages 14-15.*

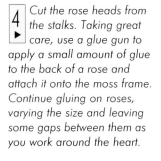

2 ▲ *Bend a wire clothes hanger (or a thick piece of wire) into a heart shape and twist the ends as shown. Trim the excess with wire cutters.*

3 ▶ *Take a handful of the dried moss and wind it loosely around the wire. Knot a length of jute or string at the starting point and then wind it around the moss, binding it in place. Continue working around the heart, adding more moss as required and binding it with string.*

4 ▶ *Cut the rose heads from the stalks. Taking great care, use a glue gun to apply a small amount of glue to the back of a rose and attach it onto the moss frame. Continue gluing on roses, varying the size and leaving some gaps between them as you work around the heart.*

5 ◀ *Cut hydrangea flowers and apply a small amount of glue to the back of each with the glue gun. Use a toothpick or other implement to press them onto the frame so that your fingers do not touch the hot glue. Decorate the sides and fill any gaps between the roses in this way.*

PROJECT 21

Door Wreath

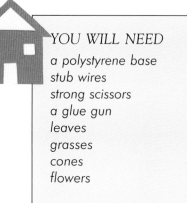

YOU WILL NEED
a polystyrene base
stub wires
strong scissors
a glue gun
leaves
grasses
cones
flowers

This rustic wreath captures the beauty of late summer. Its warm, earthy colors and abundant foliage will grace any door or wall in your home.

1 ◄ Dry the flowers (we have used yarrow, safflower, hydrangeas and yellow helichrysum), leaves and grasses (such as wheat and quaking grass), as instructed on pages 14-15. Cones and flowers with weak stalks will need to be wired individually.

2 ▲ Bend stub wires and cut them to form long staples. Use these to pin dried leaves onto the polystyrene base, overlapping them so that none of the base is visible. Make sure the sides are also covered.

3 ▲ Use stub wires to tie small bundles of grasses and sprays of flowers.

4 ◄ Stick the wired bundles onto the wreath base, evenly spacing each type of plant material. Cover the top and sides so that the wreath has a rounded shape.

5 ► Insert the cones and the individually wired flowers as features around the wreath. These should jut out a bit further than the background foliage and blossoms. Make sure that all wires have been covered.

Potpourri

It is hard to believe that anything as delightful as potpourri could bear a name which translates literally as "rotten pot". Originally it referred to a pot of meat and vegetable stock but during the eighteenth century it came to mean flowers mixed to ward off diseases and mask unpleasant odors. In large houses, the mixing of potpourri was a serious if pleasant responsibility and a distilling room was dedicated to this and related tasks. These days, potpourris are more of a joy than a necessity, but bringing the aromas of the garden into the home has great rewards.

Traditionally, potpourris were based on fragrant rose petals. This is still commonly the case, but other scented flowers such as lavender, jasmine, and honeysuckle are also used, along with scented geranium leaves and other foliage. Herbs and freshly-ground spices are the next main ingredients, together with other non-floral elements such as dried citrus peel. A few drops of an essential oil matching the flowers is added to strengthen the scent. Finally, all potpourri recipes call for a fixative, an ingredient which absorbs and holds the scent. This element was originally an animal product—civet, musk or the like—but has been replaced with such vegetable matters as orris root or gum benzoin. These are available in most health food or craft stores but nutmeg and cinnamon powder also have fixative properties and can be substituted. For pure aesthetics, you can also include unscented flowers, berries, small cones or cinnamon sticks.

There are two basic methods for making potpourris: moist and dry. These are outlined on the next page. The first produces a more potent but less visually appealing mix; the latter is quicker.

Potpourris can be displayed in open bowls or boxes, or in a container with a perforated lid. Alternatively, you can fill sachets with potpourri and store them among clothes and linen or anything else you wish to scent.

Rose & lavender
Here is a simple recipe for a dry potpourri:
3 tbsps orris root powder
2 drops rosemary oil
2 drops rose oil
4 cups rose petals
½ cup lavender
½ cup oak moss
2 tbsps rosemary

1 To make the base for a moist potpourri, layer partially dried rose petals with coarse salt in a jar. Petal layers should be three times the thickness of each salt layer. Seal the jar and store in a dark place for three weeks while the contents cure.

If using the dry method, simply dry rose petals fully.

2 For either type of potpourri, mix the spices and a fixative such as orris root powder or gum benzoin. Add drops of a floral oil and mix it in with the fingertips.

Potpourris made by the moist method are not especially attractive. Containers with a perforated lid such as this one are a good means of displaying them.

3 Combine the larger ingredients of the potpourri: the dried petals (or the cured petal base of a moist potpourri) with the spice mixture. Store the potpourri in an airtight container for a month before arranging it in a bowl or open box.

Attractive flowers which have little or no scent can be added to a potpourri for decoration.

PROJECT 22

Spices & Citrus

This combination of bright colors and tangy aromas makes a stunning potpourri which is particularly suitable for freshening bathrooms or kitchens.

1 ▶ Collect yellow flowers such as marigolds and yarrow and some leaves (we have used eucalyptus leaves). Dry the flowers and leaves as instructed on pages 14-15. Cut strips of peel from such fruits as lemons, limes, oranges and grapefruit. Dry the strips in a warm oven.

2 ▲ In a bowl, combine ¼ cup of orris root powder with 1 teaspoon each of nutmeg, cloves, cardamom and coriander. Add five drops of lemon oil and mix the ingredients with your fingers.

3 ▲ Leave some flower heads to one side. In another bowl, combine the citrus peel, leaves, cinnamon sticks and remaining flowers. Add the spice mixture and combine thoroughly.

4 ▶ Put the potpourri mix in an airtight container and lay the reserved flowers on top. Store this in a dark place for several weeks so that the scents develop fully.

5 ▶ Put the potpourri into a wooden container. Add kumquats if available. Turn the citrus peel colored side up and arrange the reserved flowers attractively on top.

PROJECT 23

Potpourri Sachets

These elegant bags are quick to prepare and a delight to give. They can be filled with any highly scented potpourri, such as a lavender or rose petal mix.

YOU WILL NEED
orris root powder
scented flowers
floral oil
an airtight container
organza fabric
gold thread
pinking shears
needle & thread
scissors

1 ▶ Dry the flowers as shown on pages 14-15. When they are quite dry, gently remove the petals or flower heads from the stems: to fill two sacks you will need 10 tablespoons of dried flowers.

2 ▶ Mix 1 teaspoon of orris root powder and 6 drops of a suitable floral oil. Add the dried flowers and mix the ingredients thoroughly. If time allows, put the potpourri in an airtight container and store it in a dark place for several weeks to allow the scent to develop.

3 ◀ Cut a 7 " square of organza fabric with pinking shears so that the raw edges do not fray. Fold the fabric in half and sew a seam along the base and the raw side. Turn the opening over and sew a deep hem. Turn the bag inside out.

4 ▶ Fill the bag two-thirds full with the potpourri. Tie the opening tightly with gold thread and then tie a bow over the knot.

PROJECT 24

Christaras Mix

This festive potpourri is made by the moist method, which creates a rich perfume. Prepare it well before Christmas and store it away afterwards for use in many future years.

YOU WILL NEED
red roses
coarse salt
ivy leaves
glycerin
dried moss
small cones & pods
juniper berries
rose oil & pine oil
cinnamon
orris root powder

1 Remove enough red rose petals to fill a large bowl and spread them on newspaper. Place in a warm spot for several days until they are leathery but are not yet fully dried. Immerse ivy leaves in a solution of equal parts boiling water and glycerin for a week. Rinse the preserved leaves under a faucet and wipe dry.

2 Reserve some large petals for decoration. In an airtight jar, layer the remaining partially dried petals and coarse salt. Each petal layer should be three times thicker than the layer of salt. Seal the jar and store in a dark place for three weeks.

3 Mix 2 tablespoons orris root powder and 1 tablespoon cinnamon. Add five drops of rose oil and rub it in. In a large bowl mix the cured petals, dried moss and 1 tablespoon lightly crushed juniper berries. Store the potpourri in an airtight container for a month.

4 Working out of doors, spray small cones and pods with gold spray paint. Pine oil may be painted under the "leaves" of the cones for added scent.

5 Place the potpourri in an attractive bowl and decorate the top with the large petals, along with the preserved ivy leaves and gold painted cones.

Scented Gifts

One of the joys of flowers is the unique aroma that many of them bear, which allows you to close your eyes and still see the blossoms clearly. Transferring that fragrance onto a gift is almost like doubling its value. Scents are not simply aesthetic, many have medicinal qualities. The smell of lavender, for example, has the power to soothe, while that of rosemary can make you feel invigorated. Many friends will have a favorite scent; if you discover it, make a note and treat them to a gift carrying that fragrance when next you give them a present.

Natural materials will hold a scent best. Paper can be scented by sprinkling a potpourri between sheets and storing it awhile. Gift wrapping, stationery, drawer liners, and cards are just a few of the things that can be made extra special by this method. Lavender can be sprinkled onto the wadding used when making a padded clothes hanger, or sewn into the lining of toilet bags or lingerie cases. As an alternative to sprinkling loose petals, you can make small scented sachets. Choose light fabrics made of natural fibers, such as cotton, which allow the scent to escape through the weave. Filled with aromatic mixtures, these make sweet gifts and can be stored amongst clothes, linen or books. Small pillows filled with a rose petal and violet potpourri encourage sleep and make a thoughtful present.

Another enjoyable way to release a floral scent is by burning a perfumed candle, and a home-made one is a most delightful gift. Project 27 provides instructions for making and decorating candles.

Where practical, match the scent to the color of the item: rose fragrance for red or pink, lavender for blue or purple, jasmine or magnolia for white, and so on. Crushing flowers will help to release their scent. If you require a stronger perfume, add a few drops of an essential oil or apply it with a cotton bud. This is also a good way to refresh a scent which has faded with time.

Fabric and paper items can be scented with a floral fragrance to make a special gift.

AROMATIC FLOWERS

Here are some of the many flowers that bear a delicious scent.

Alkanet - *Anchusa officinalis*
Carnation - *Dianthus caryophyllus*
Chamomile - *Matricaria recutica*
Freesia - *Freesia x kewensis*
Golden-rayed lily - *Lilium auratum*
Honeysuckle - *Lonicera periclymenum*
Hops - *Humulus lupulus*
Hyacinth - *Hyacinthus*
Iris - *Iridaceae*
Jasmine - *Jasminum officinale*
Lavender - *Lavandula vera*
Lilac - *Syringa*
Lily of the valley - *Convallaria*
Lime flower - *Tilia europaea*
Magnolia - *Magnolia grandiflora*
Mimosa - *Acacia dealbata*
Mock orange - *Philadelphus* species
Orange blossom - *Citrus sinensis*
Peony - *Paeonia lactiflora*
Pinks - *Dianthus caryophyllus*
Red clover - *Trifolium pratense*
Rose - *Rosa gallica*
Stock - *Matthiola incana*
Sweet pea - *Lathyrus*
Sweet William - *Dianthus barbatus*
Tansy - *Tanacetum vulgare*
Thyme - *Thymus vulgaris*
Violet - *Viola odorata*
Wallflower - *Cheiranthus cheiri*
Woodruff - *Asperula odorata*

Rosary beads
Traditionally used for devotional prayers, these scented beads are made from rose petals which have been mashed into a pulp. Roll the pulp into balls, pierce each one with a pin and allow them to harden. When the beads are firm, polish them with rose oil.

PROJECT 25

Lavender Bottles

YOU WILL NEED

lavender
ribbon
a knife
scissors

Lavender stems can be bent back to form a "bottle" around the flower heads, making delightful gifts which will keep linen and handkerchiefs smelling sweet.

1 ◄ Collect 22 long stems of fresh or dried lavender, preferably French lavender which has a well-defined flower head. Use a knife or your fingertips to strip off any foliage below the flower head. Cut 60 " of ribbon and tie one end tightly around the bunch, just below the flower heads.

2 ◄ Turn the bunch upside down and bend each stem down over the ribbon. If you are using dried stems which are brittle, hold a damp sponge to the neck before bending the stem.

3 ► Weave the long end of the ribbon under a pair of stems and over the next pair. Repeat this, working around the flower heads. Weave tightly at the top and bottom and more loosely in the middle to create the bottle shape and to prevent any flowers from falling out.

4 ◄ Knot the ribbon tightly around the neck of the "bottle" and tie a bow over the knot. Trim the ends of the stems evenly.

PROJECT 26

Lining Paper

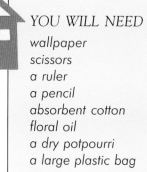

Scented lining paper is an attractive way to keep cupboards and drawers smelling fresh. Vary the ingredients of the floral mix according to your own tastes.

1 Make up a dry potpourri as shown on page 73. A suggested recipe is: 2 parts rose petals, 1 part lavender, 1 part jasmine flowers, 2 drops patchouli oil, 2 tablespoons orris powder or other fixative.

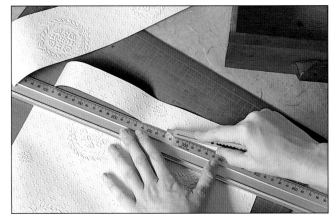

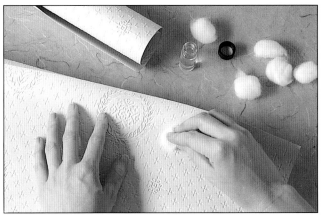

2 Select a wallpaper which is not pre-pasted and which will absorb a scent. Measure the dimensions of the shelves or drawers and cut sheets of wallpaper to the desired size.

3 Put a few drops of floral oil (complementing the floral mixture) on an absorbent cotton ball and wipe the unpatterned side of a lining paper. Refresh the cotton ball for each sheet.

4 Sprinkle the floral mixture thickly on the patterned side of a liner paper. Lay another sheet on top and sprinkle with more mixture. Repeat for each of the papers.

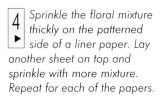

5 Roll the layers together and seal the roll in the large plastic bag. Leave in a warm, dark place for a month so that the liners absorb the scent. The floral mixture can later be used to fill sachets or a potpourri bowl. Weight the liners until they lie flat.

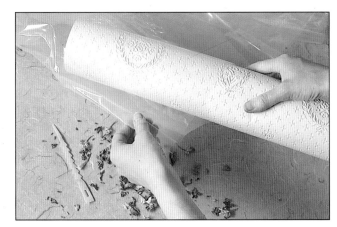

PROJECT 27

Scented Candles

Candle molds can be bought or improvized using household items. You can use any container that will hold hot wax and from which the finished candle can be removed.

YOU WILL NEED

paraffin wax
stearin
wicks
plastic bottles
masking tape
modeling clay
floral oil
kitchen utensils
pressed flowers
a brush

1 ▶ Cut the top off a plastic bottle and make two cuts down the sides. Dip a wick of suitable thickness in melted wax. When it is cool, tie one end around a skewer. Lay this wick rod over the opening of the mold. Thread the wick through a hole in the other end and secure it with modeling clay. Tape up the sides and around the mold.

2 ▶ Melt the paraffin wax in a bowl over a saucepan of water. Melt the stearin, a hardening agent, in another saucepan; you will need 1 part stearin to every 9 parts wax. Add a few drops of floral oil to the stearin and then add this mixture to the melted wax. Stir to combine.

3 ◀ Pour the mixture slowly into the upright mold. Tap it gently to release any air bubbles. After an hour, a depression will have formed around the wick. Break the skin with a skewer and top it up with more melted wax. When the candle is quite cool, remove it by tapping the mold.

4 ◀ Smooth the seams of the candle with a knife. Smooth the base by holding it over a heated saucepan. To decorate the candle, arrange pressed flowers around the lower section and brush on melted wax to secure them in place. Do not leave decorated candles burning unattended as the flowers may ignite.

Pressed Flowers

One of the most enjoyable ways to preserve flowers is by pressing them. Whether the subject is a lavish wedding bouquet or a single meadow flower picked on a walk, a pressed arrangement can bring back delightful memories.

Apart from the obvious difference of being flat, pressed flowers can differ in other ways from their three-dimensional counterparts. The process of pressing can alter a flower's color significantly, reducing or intensifying it, or even changing it altogether. The shape can also be changed: some shapes will become more distinctive, others will lose their definition and be less identifiable. The best way to learn is to press a wide variety of flowers and study the results.

Fresh flowers should be gathered when they are dry and all dew has evaporated. Press them as soon as possible after picking. Dried flowers can be pressed if they are first held over steam briefly. Various parts of a plant can be pressed: the leaves, blossoms, buds and some types of fruit are all worth attempting.

Sprays of flowers can often be pressed whole, but some will need to be separated into single blooms and pressed individually.

Similarly, simple, delicate flowers can generally be pressed flat but more complex ones may need to be removed from the stalk and the layers of petals carefully thinned.

Once they have been prepared, flowers can be pressed between the pages of a large book. However, a more effective result will be obtained if you use a purpose-made flower press. This need not be especially large or expensive. The best ones are those that can be tightened at various points and so will press the flowers evenly. Instructions for making a flower press are given on page 11.

Flowers should be placed between two sheets of blotting paper (or other absorbent paper) and placed in the press. Try to keep sections of the same plant together, although each layer should contain material of roughly the same thickness. It is a good idea to label each layer with the date of pressing and the name of the plant. Leave material in the press for approximately six weeks.

Use tweezers to handle the pressed flowers and apply craft glue to each one with a toothpick before placing them in a design. The possibilities for using pressed flowers are almost endless: the projects in this chapter offer just a few ideas to get you started.

◄ Bulky or fleshy sections will be difficult to press. Some, such as rosebuds, can be sliced in half with a sharp knife and then pressed.

These pansies were dismantled for pressing and then reassembled.

◄ Complex flowers may be carefully pulled apart and each of the petals pressed separately. These can then be reconstructed in your design.

Candles can be decorated with delicate flowers and leaves which will glow when the candle is lit. Glue the pressed flowers near the base where they will not be burned and brush a thin coating of melted wax over them.

Posies of miniature country flowers make a lovely framed display. Such arrangements are often visited by tiny insects, so give your finished project a brief spray with a household insecticide.

PROJECT 28

Pressed Sampler

Samplers are an ideal introduction to the art of pressing flowers and provide a lovely decoration for a kitchen or living room. A variety of flowers could be displayed in a larger frame.

1 ▶ Select a wooden frame which has a natural finish. New wood can be 'aged' by denting it with a set of keys and lightly sanding it before varnishing. Cut a piece of card or paper to fit into the recess of the frame.

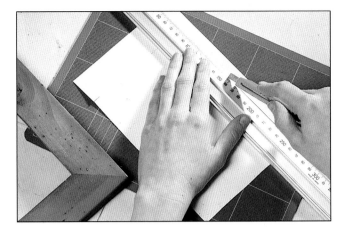

2 ▶ Choose a plant that has interesting leaves and flower petals; we have used viola tricolor (commonly known as heart's-ease). Carefully press the leaves, flower heads and stalks (see pages 88-89). You may wish to press a section of the root as well.

3 ◀ Once the plant material is fully dried, remove it from the press. Arrange the plant sections on the card in the shape of the plant. Glue them in place with a small amount of craft glue.

4 ◀ Use a calligraphy pen to write the botanical or common name (or both) of the plant. When the ink is dry, place the sampler in the prepared frame.

PROJECT 29

Festive Card

With just a few flowers and a touch of gold paint you can make a beautiful card for someone special. Here they have formed a Christmas tree, but the idea can be adapted for any occasion.

YOU WILL NEED
a flower press
fern leaves
feathery sprays
small red flowers
gold spray paint
small beads
tweezers
craft glue
white card
a ruler, knife & mat

1 ◄ Press the flowers and leaves as described on page 88. Cut a rectangle of white card. Score a line down the center so that it folds neatly in half to form a greeting card. Glue overlapping fern leaves on the card in the shape of a fir tree and add several stems as a trunk.

2 ◄ Place the pressed feathery sprays (we have used cow parsley or Queen Anne's lace) and the small beads on newspaper and spray them with gold paint. When dry, break off florets of the cow parsley and glue some onto the fern as shown.

3 ◄ Glue pressed red flowers onto the card, with one covering the tip of the tree. Dip the gold beads in glue and add them to the design.

4 ► Break off extra florets of cow parsley which have been sprayed with gold paint. Arrange them around the edge of the card to form a border, gluing them in place as you work.

Suggestion: If you plan to send this card through the post, you can protect the design by covering the card with a clear self-adhesive plastic.

PROJECT 30

Paperweight

Make a paperweight that is worthy of any desk. This delicate pot of bright flowers would also add a nice touch to a box lid, a greeting card or any small project.

YOU WILL NEED

a flower press
small flowers
dark leaves
light-colored card
a compass
a knife & mat
craft glue
tweezers
a toothpick
a glass paperweight

1 ▶ *Press several dark leaves (such as copper beech or prunus) and a selection of very small flowers (see pages 88-89). Those used here include forget-me-nots, cow parsley, fuchsia, pansies, miniature rosebuds and sea lavender. Cut a piece of card to fit the recess of the bought paperweight.*

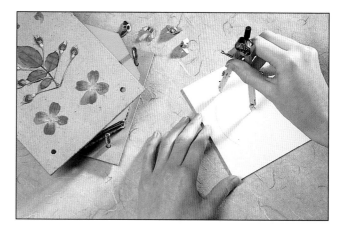

2 ◀ *Once the plant materials are fully dried, remove them from the press. Cut sections of the leaves to form a pot and glue them onto the card with a small amount of craft glue.*

3 ▲ *Glue down several small pieces of foliage to mark the edges of the arrangement. Add florets of cow parsley and sea lavender, then fill any gaps with small flower heads.*

4 ▶ *Insert the disk of card with the finished flower pot in the recess of the paperweight and seal it in place with the cover provided.*

Coated Flowers

Fresh flowers have a delicate quality that is often sacrificed when they are dried or pressed. There are other ways of extending the life of blooms so that they can be used for decoration. Some edible methods, such as frosting, crystallizing and glazing, are considered in the later chapter, "Sweet Flowers". In this section we look at various other methods for capturing the beauty of flowers.

Few things are more attractive than flowers suspended in ice. Project 32 shows how to make an ice bowl, ideal for serving drinks and chilled desserts. Alternatively, you could make a flower-filled ice cooler for bottles, or simple ice cubes, each containing an edible flower (a list of such flowers appears on page 145). Flowers trapped in Jell-o or a thin layer of gelatin also look appealing. While on the subject of floral fare, try half-dipping red rose petals in melted dark chocolate for a dramatic decoration.

Dried flowers which have lost their color can be given a coating of spray paint. A very light coat of white paint gives a display a winter frosting and is ideal for outdoor arrangements. Gold, silver and red are all suitable colors for Christmas. Make sure the flowers and foliage have interesting shapes and textures—helichrysum, holly leaves and seed-heads such as nigella or poppies look particularly effective—and allow some of the original colors to peek through. Spray paints should be used in a well-ventilated area, preferably out of doors.

To give dried flowers the full treatment, you can apply a heavy coat of white paint and then create your own color variations, as we have done in Project 33. If your dried flowers can't cope with this sort of treatment, a similar effect can be achieved by coating bought fabric flowers with a fabric stiffener and then painting them as we have done.

Sprays of dried flowers are often dyed before being sold. This sometimes creates a garish appearance, but can add a touch of color.

A quick spray of gold paint can give faded dried flowers a second lease of life.

A thin coating of wax can extend the life of some blooms and enhance leaves. Melt paraffin wax over a very low heat. Test the wax by dipping leaves; if the wax sizzles it is too hot for dipping flowers. Let it cool slightly and dip flower heads into the wax. Lay them on wax paper and let them set.

Small flowers or petals can be added when making paper. Dry or press the flowers first, then mix them into the paper pulp. As the sheet is formed on the mesh mold, the flowers will be trapped in the pulp. A second dip into the pulp will embed them and ensure they are secure.

PROJECT 31

Gilt Decorations

These gilded pieces make stunning ornaments on the Christmas tree. A simpler version, without wiring, could be used to decorate presents.

1 ▶ Select dried flowers which have an interesting shape; we have used helichrysum (also known as everlastings). For more information on wiring, see page 13. Select small ivy leaves which have long stems and are in good condition.

2 ▶ Lay the flowers and leaves on a sheet of newspaper outside and spray them with gold paint. Turn the leaves when dry and spray over the backs as well.

3 ▶ Cut a strip of card 2 " wide and lay a short piece of cotton twine along it. Wind another length of cotton twine around it 20 times. Tie the ends of the short piece together so that the loops are gathered tightly. Slip them off the card and wind a gold thread tightly around the neck of the tassel. Cut the unbound ends of the loops.

4 ◀ Hold the leaves and a flower together and bind them with stem tape. Tie the tassels loosely onto the wire behind the flower head. Use the tape-covered wire to attach the decoration to a tree branch.

PROJECT 32

Floral Ice Bowl

YOU WILL NEED
two bowls
a heavy jar
an ice-cube tray
fresh flowers
leaves

Flowers trapped in ice make an enchanting serving bowl for drinks or ice cream. It is best to make it in stages as the flowers will naturally float to the top.

1 ▶ You will need two freezer-proof bowls, one smaller than the other. In the larger bowl, pour water to a depth of 1 " and place the bowl in a freezer for several hours.

2 ▶ Collect non-poisonous fresh flowers and leaves: we have used hydrangeas and nasturtiums. Other edible flowers are listed on page 145. Place the small bowl in the larger one and push plant material into the gap. Weigh the small bowl down with a heavy jar and add water to a third of the height. Return this to the freezer.

3 ▶ Add another layer of flowers and water and refreeze. Fill the bowl with water to just below the rim and freeze overnight. To remove the ice bowl, pour cold water into the smaller bowl and wait until the bowls separate easily.

4 ▶ To make floral ice-cubes, place a flower in each section of a tray and fill with water. Leave the tray in the freezer for half an hour. Break each icy covering with a fork, and push the floating flower down into the cube. Return the tray to the freezer and allow the blocks to freeze completely.

PROJECT 33

Porcelain Roses

*One of the few drawbacks of dried flowers is their fragility.
The process used here gives blooms added durability while
hinting at the delicate appearance of porcelain pieces.*

1 ◄ Select dried flower heads which are well shaped and stems with leaves which are not overly curled. Working out of doors, spray flowers and leaves with white paint. Allow these to dry and spray with a second coat.

2 ► Paint the leaves and sepals in pale green. When this coat is dry, paint lines of dark green along the center of each leaf and blur the lines with water. Paint the flower heads so that the tips and bases of the petals vary in shade.

3 ► When the painted flowers and leaves are dry, apply a coat of acrylic varnish, covering both sides of each leaf. Leave to dry and apply a second coat.

4 ► Paint a box with several coats of cream paint. Arrange the flowers and leaves on the lid before using a glue gun to fix them in the desired position.

Suggestion: Fabric flowers can also be decorated in this way, but should be dipped in fabric stiffener before being painted.

Paper Creations

The appeal of flowers is so strong that we are forever trying to recreate them around us, either in painting or embroidery, in porcelain or sugarpaste. Of all the materials available to us, paper is among the least expensive and has the most potential.

When we turn to paper, we are really looking at various types of fiber with quite different properties. Crêpe paper, available in many shades and hues, has an inherent elasticity which allows you to sculpt realistic petals and leaves. Fine tissue paper is ideal for making delicate fronds and flowers, such as carnations or cornflowers. Stiff construction paper serves to make stylized shapes, akin to origami flowers made traditionally in Japan. Twisted paper ribbon, now widely available, is inherently strong and has interesting creases which can become part of the flower design.

If you have a range of papers on hand, you can experiment as much as you please.

Choose a flower, or a picture of a flower, as a model and study it closely.

Decide which type of paper will best suit its features. Should it be represented accurately or in an abstract fashion? If you're trying to mimic it, look at the stamens and calyx and consider how they can be recreated. Will the heads need to be mounted on wire stems or can they be arranged in a shallow bowl?

If you cannot match the color with the available papers, consider coloring a white paper with watercolor paint or adding markings with a crayon. A light application of a spray paint may be a possible solution.

Minimal equipment is needed to make paper flowers. Small pointed scissors or pinking shears are useful for serrating the edges of petals and leaves. Stem tape is needed to conceal wires, or you can wind strips of paper around them and secure the ends with tape or glue. White glue, a craft knife and a cutting board are all useful.

Making paper flowers is a fun and rewarding pastime. The results can be used to decorate gifts, adorn a hat or simply to brighten that awkward corner of a room.

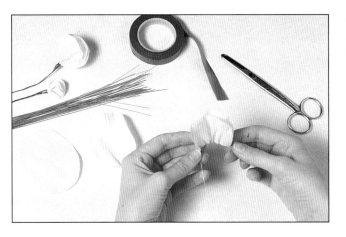

To make sweet peas, cut two ovals in crêpe paper so that the natural creases run along the long diagonal. Carefully stretch the edges at the top and bottom of each oval. Place the ovals together and lay a wire across the shortest diagonal. Bend the wire so that the petals are gathered and twist the wire to secure. Wind absorbent cotton around the base to form a calyx and then cover it and the stem with tape.

Sunflower

Twisted paper ribbon has been used to make this dramatic sunflower. Cut long strips of brown or rust ribbon and fold them in half lengthways. Working along the unfolded edge, make a series of snips two-thirds of the way down towards the fold. Roll this section into a coil, gluing on more pieces until you have a large flower center. Cut petals from yellow ribbon so that the creases run top to bottom and glue them around the rolled center.

Wreath of roses

Perhaps the most popular of paper flowers are crêpe paper roses. Instructions for making these can be found on page 111.

PROJECT 34

Breezy Daffodils

YOU WILL NEED
colored papers
tracing paper
a pencil
a knife & mat
glue
a pot
moss or fiber

Spring can flourish all year-round with this ingenious display of daffodils. A few blooms make a delightful decoration in a baby's room or a child's bedroom.

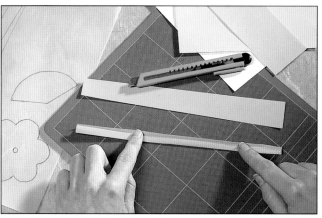

1 For each bloom, trace the pattern sections onto colored paper and cut a trumpet and stamen, a petal collar, a stem and a leaf. Cut a frill along the trumpet edge. Fold the leaves lengthways along the dashed line. Fold the stem along the dashed lines and glue the overlapping edge to form a long triangular shape.

2 Shape the white collar: score lightly with a knife along the dashed lines, turn the paper over and score lightly along the dotted lines. Fold along the scored lines to form the cup shape. Thread this onto the stem. Cut and roll the stamens then glue them into the tip of the stem.

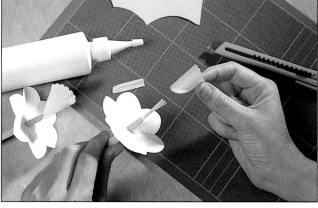

3 Roll and glue the trumpet section into a cylinder. Thread this over the stamens and glue it onto the stem. Push the white collar over the trumpet and glue it at the back. Put moss or coconut fiber in a pot and arrange the daffodils and leaves in place.

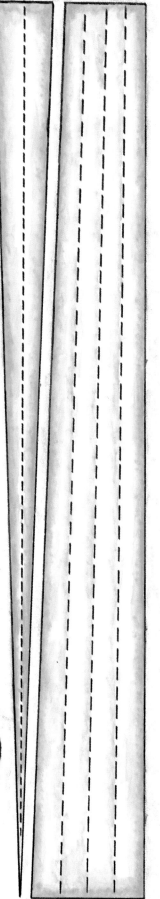

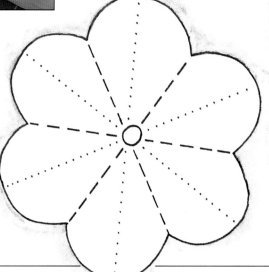

PROJECT 35

Cornflower Spray

YOU WILL NEED

blue tissue paper
green tissue paper
a pencil
a compass
pinking shears
stem tape
stub wires
absorbent cotton
glue

The lovely blue of these paper cornflowers will cheer up anyone who is not feeling well. The same pattern can be used to make pink or white cornflowers.

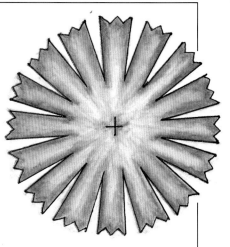

1 Mark circles onto blue tissue paper: each flower requires three large circles and three small ones. Cut out the circles with pinking shears or zigzag the edges. Fold each paper circle into sixteen segments by folding in half, unfolding, turning, folding, and so on. Snip a dart between each fold and cut an "x" in the center. The piece should now look like the diagram.

2 Crumple a small piece of blue tissue paper into a ball and thread it onto a stub wire. Bend the wire to secure the paper ball, which forms the center of the flower.

3 Dab some glue at the back of the flower center. Thread a small petal circle onto the wire so that it rests behind the flower center. Dab glue behind the petal circle and thread on the next one. Repeat, using all three small circles and then the three large ones.

4 Bind some absorbent cotton around the wire behind the last petal circle to form a calyx. Bind this with stem tape and continue winding the stem tape to cover the stem. Make enough flowers for a posy and cut long leaves from green tissue paper. Decorate the posy with a ribbon bow.

PROJECT 36

Crêpe Roses

A small basket or vase of delicate roses is a perfect gift for Mother's Day, especially if the flowers have been handmade with loving attention.

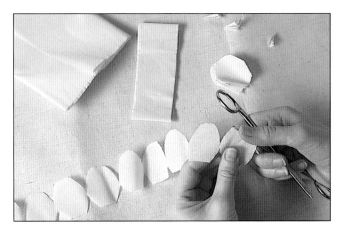

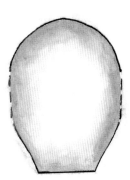

1 Cut a long strip of pink crêpe paper across the grain (so the grain lines run top to bottom) and pleat it to form ten layers. Cut a petal shape from the layers, leaving the sides uncut to create a chain of petals. Curl the petal tops outwards by drawing them over the blade of the scissors. Stretch each petal across its width.

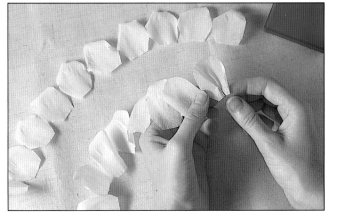

2 Pierce the lower part of an end petal with a stub wire, then twist the wire to secure it. Wrap the petal chain around the wire quite tightly, gathering each petal at the base. Secure the last petal in the chain with a small piece of adhesive tape.

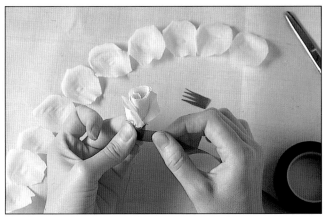

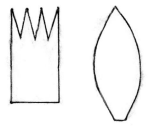

3 Cut a 1" piece of stem tape and snip darts at one end to form the sepal. Stretch it across so that it fits around the base of the paper rose. Secure it in place by binding around the base with stem tape. Continue binding at an angle so that the wire is fully wrapped.

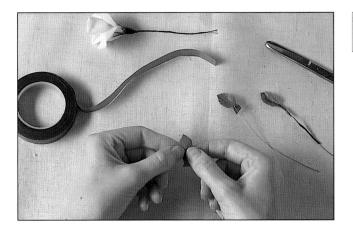

4 Cut a leaf shape from stem tape and serrate the edges with sharp scissors. Stretch the tape across the leaf to create a central vein. Pierce the base with a stub wire and twist the wire to secure. Bind the wire with stem tape. Arrange roses and leaves in a small vase and decorate with a ribbon bow.

Fabric Flowers

The art of forming flowers from fabric became popular several decades ago. Most early examples drew praise for the patience of their makers rather than for any particular realism. These days, however, an abundance of artificial flowers are available commercially and many are hard to distinguish from their garden-grown counterparts. The advantages of using such creations in arrangements are several: your choice of flowers isn't restricted by the season, you can choose any type of container, and the flowers will need dusting rather than replacing. Though fabric flowers can never fully replace fresh ones, they may well have a place in your home, especially if you have made them yourself.

The projects in this chapter introduce several different methods. The felt poinsettia is made with concealed wires to give petals and leaves their shape. If you wish to use a lighter fabric to make large flowers, you can strengthen it by applying a starch solution which will also prevent the edges from fraying. Ribbon roses are made by rolling a single piece of fabric rather than by piecing together individual petals and are very quick to make once you've mastered the skill. The third project, silk freesias, offers an introduction to the techniques of painting silk and constructing more complex blossoms. A whole world of flower-making awaits anyone prepared to explore the possibilities of this art by matching nature with subtle gradations of color.

Flowers can be made from a range of fabrics: experiment with scraps before cutting numerous petals. Artificial stamens, which can add authenticity, are available from craft supply stores. You can buy them in different colors, but a good alternative is to buy white ones and tint them to suit your project.

Making foliage from fabric is less rewarding and it is a good idea to complement your fabric flowers with foliage preserved in glycerin or with fresh foliage which can be replaced when necessary.

1 ◄ To make a ribbon rose, start by folding one end of the ribbon towards you to form a stem. Roll the stem back along the ribbon and continue rolling until you have formed the center of the rose.

2 ► Fold the unrolled length of ribbon towards you but do not crease the fold. Roll the center of the rose along the fold at an angle, so that the ribbon flares out to form a petal shape. When you reach the end of the fold, repeat this step.

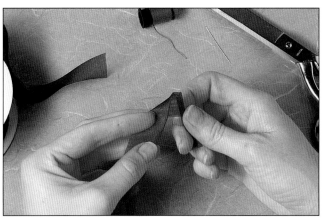

3 ◄ When the rose is the desired size, taper the ribbon down towards the stem. Pierce the stem with several stitches, making sure that the rose is secure and will not collapse. Trim the ends of the ribbon.

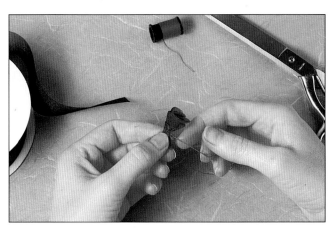

Wire flowers
Bend fine wire into loops and twist to secure. Stretch nylon stocking fabric over each loop and tie with thread to form a petal. Arrange six petals with stamens, bind with wire and cover with stem tape.

Velvet pansies
Cut two petal sections from velvet and apply white glue around the edges to prevent fraying. Paint ready-made stamens yellow and push them through the two petal sections. Gather the flower at the back and bind with a stub wire.

PROJECT 37

Felt Poinsettia

YOU WILL NEED
colored felt
a pencil
scrap paper
scissors
stub wires
stem tape
glue
absorbent cotton

This bright flower makes an unusual decoration at Christmas time. Use it to adorn a special gift or as the feature on a wreath of dark leaves.

1 ▶ Cut a paper template to match each pattern on the right. Use these templates to cut 14 small petals and 6 large petals from red felt. Glue the shapes together in pairs with a stub wire sandwiched between the sections. As a result, you should have 7 small petals and 3 large petals.

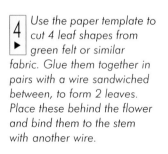

2 ◀ Cut a small triangle of felt, pierce it with a stub wire. Bend the wire over and cover it with stem tape to form a stamen. Make 8 red and 4 yellow stamens, then bind them together in a bundle with an extra wire.

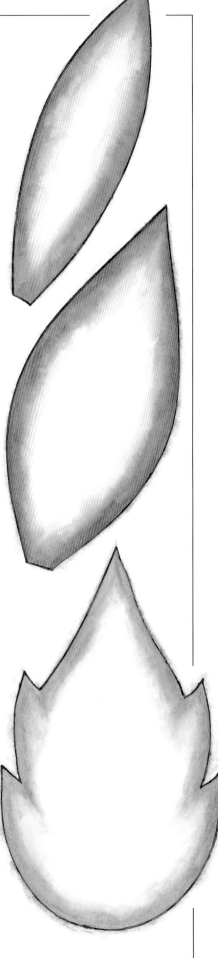

3 ▶ Arrange the small petals around the stamen bundle and then add the larger petals. Bind them together tightly at the neck with a wire. Wrap a piece of absorbent cotton around the wire and cover it with stem tape, winding the tape down the stem of wires.

4 ▶ Use the paper template to cut 4 leaf shapes from green felt or similar fabric. Glue them together in pairs with a wire sandwiched between, to form 2 leaves. Place these behind the flower and bind them to the stem with another wire.

PROJECT 38

Ribbon Hair Clip

YOU WILL NEED

wide ribbons
a needle
sewing thread
scissors
thick card
velvet fabric
a hair clip
a glue gun

Ribbon roses lend an air of old-fashioned elegance to whatever they adorn. This hair clip, boasting a posy of roses, would make a delightful gift for a girl.

1 ◄ Measure the length of your hair clip and cut a rectangle of heavy card slightly longer than the clip. Trim the corners to create an oval base.

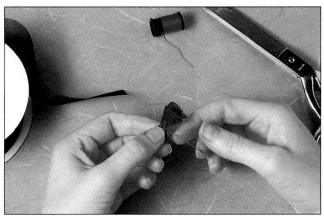

2 ◄ Roll seven roses in two complementary colors of ribbon. See page 113 for full instructions. We have used a crimson organza ribbon and a pale pink satin ribbon. Both have been folded lengthwise for added fulness.

3 ► Cut a square of velvet (or crushed velvet) twice the length of your card oval. Fold it in half with right sides together and tuck the roses inside the pocket of fabric. Stitch along the fold, securing the roses in place. Make sure that when you unfold the velvet square, the stems are concealed.

4 ► Glue the card base onto the wrong side of the velvet square so that the roses sit over it. Use the glue gun to secure the fabric on the back of the base. Trim the excess velvet and glue the clip on top.

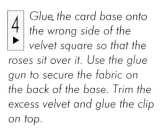

PROJECT 39

Silk Freesias

These delicate silk flowers are a work of art and can be made quite quickly after a little practice. Choose a tightly woven silk that won't fray easily when cut.

YOU WILL NEED
white silk
silk paints
a brush
a pencil
scissors
a spoon or skewer
stub wires
stem tape
a towel

1 Wet the silk and lay it on scrap paper. Paint the whole piece yellow and then add an orange tint along the bottom third. Allow the fabric to dry. Use the patterns below to mark petal shapes in pencil; for a freesia spray you will need one flower in each size. Cut out the petal sections.

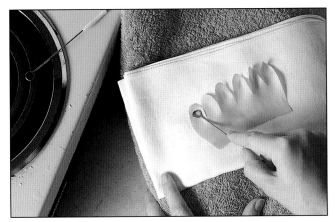

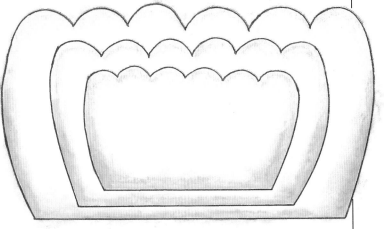

2 Lay the petal section on a cloth or towel. Heat an old teaspoon, skewer handle, or other rounded object and press it onto the top center of each petal to form a cupped shape.

3 Roll the base of the flower loosely and then bind it with a fine stub wire. Cover the wire by wrapping it with green stem tape. Make each of the three flowers in this way.

4 To make a bud, cut a triangle of painted silk and fold it inwards several times so the raw edges are concealed. Bind it with stub wire and stem tape. Form a spray of freesias by taping a second bud to the first, and then adding the three flowers in order of increasing size.

Oils & Potions

The fragrance of a flower, and some of its other properties, can be captured and stored in a number of liquids. Water, vinegar, alcohol and oil can all be infused with flowers and then used in the kitchen or bathroom as appropriate.

Flower waters, of which rose water is the best known, can be used to flavor food or to refresh the skin and scent the body. Teas made with certain flowers can be quite delicious and beneficial—lime flowers make a soothing cup while chamomile relaxes and encourages sleep.

Floral vinegars can be added to a bath, used as a skin toner, or applied as a hair rinse after shampooing and conditioning. If made with edible and flavorsome flowers, they can also be added to salads and other dishes.

Vegetable oil infused with flowers can likewise be used in the preparation of food (see Project 49) as well as in baths (Project 41) or as the basis for some cosmetics (Project 45).

Undoubtedly, the queen of oils is a flower's essential oil, obtained through the process of distillation. Harvesting large quantities of essential oil requires complicated equipment, but small amounts can be patiently gathered by the method described on the next page. The easiest method of all is to buy small bottles of floral oil which are available in a wide range of fragrances. Only a few drops of an essential oil are needed to give a powerful scent to a project.

If, on the other hand, you are making your own infusion, remember that to create a fragrant potion, you will need to base it on a suitably fragrant flower (some are listed on page 81). Likewise, if the oil or potion is to be consumed, make sure you use edible flowers: a list of these is included on page 145.

Flower scents can be released by burning scented oil in a lamp or by adding several drops of essential oil to water which is then heated over a candle.

◄ To distill small amounts of essential oil, place fresh flower petals in a large glass jar and cover them with distilled water. Seal the jar with plastic wrap and leave it in a sunny position. When a film of oil appears on the water, lift it off with absorbent cotton and squeeze it into a small glass bottle. Continue until no more oil appears.

Flower vinegar
Steep flowers in warmed white vinegar, seal the container, leave it in the sun and shake the contents daily.

► Oil can be made fragrant by steeping petals in it. Put petals in a large glass jar, cover with an odorless vegetable oil, such as sunflower or almond, and leave in the sun for several days. Strain through cheesecloth, squeezing oil from the flowers before discarding them. Replace with fresh flowers and repeat until the oil has a strong perfume.

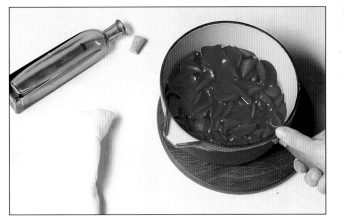

◄ To make a flower water, put fresh petals in a saucepan and cover with water. Cover the pan and simmer for 30 minutes. Cool and strain through cheesecloth, squeezing all the liquid from the petals into a glass jar.

Tisanes
Refreshing tisanes or herbal teas can be made from any edible flowers. As a guide, use a tablespoon of fresh petals or a teaspoon of dried ones per cup and allow to steep for longer than normal teas.

PROJECT 40

Jasmine Tea

YOU WILL NEED
jasmine flowers
large-leaf tea
a lemon
a knife or zest peeler
an airtight jar

In the language of flowers, jasmine means "amiability"
and what can be more amiable than sharing a cup of
fragrant tea with a good friend.

1 ▶ Cut several sprays of jasmine creeper and hang them in a warm dark place to dry. Carefully remove the dried flowers. If jasmine isn't available, substitute dried rose petals or lime flowers.

2 ▶ Cut the zest from a lemon in thin strips using a sharp knife or a zest peeler. Dry the strips of zest slowly in a warm oven or in a sunny place.

3 ▶ Measure by weight two parts of long-leaf tea, one part jasmine, and a quarter part of dried lemon zest. Combine the ingredients in a bowl.

4 ▶ Store the jasmine tea in an airtight container and decorate it if is a gift. The tea can be made either in a pot or directly in the cup. Use less than a teaspoon per cup and add a slice of lemon.

PROJECT 41

Bath Oil

YOU WILL NEED
lavender
rosemary
peppermint
sunflower oil
a mortar & pestle
an airtight jar
a saucepan
cheesecloth

This recipe requires some steeping time but the result is a fragrant oil which makes bathing a pure delight. The same concoction can be used as a hair conditioner.

1 ▶ Collect equal quantities of lavender, rosemary sprigs and peppermint leaves. Lightly bruise the fresh lavender in a mortar and pestle or by using the handle of a heavy kitchen implement.

2 ▶ Pour 2 cups of sunflower oil into a jar and add the herbs and flowers. Seal the jar tightly and place it in a sunny place or near a heater for several days. Shake the jar every day.

Suggestion: Experiment with other floral recipes for bath oils. For a sleep-inducing bath, use chamomile, lime flowers and yarrow. To ease aching muscles, use honeysuckle, hyssop, rosemary and chamomile.

3 ◀ Strain the oil through cheesecloth and squeeze any oil from the herbs and flowers. Replace them with a fresh batch of lavender, rosemary and peppermint and put the jar back in its warm place for several days. Repeat the process until the oil has a strong perfume.

4 ◀ Pour the last batch of herbs and oil into a pan and simmer it over a gentle heat for ten minutes. Allow the mixture to cool and then strain the oil into a jar. Seal the jar tightly and store in a cool, dark place. Drop a teaspoonful of oil under the running faucet of a bath.

PROJECT 42

Elderflower Fizz

This refreshing drink is ideal for celebrations on a warm summer's evening. Serve it well chilled with a slice of lemon and a sprig of mint.

1 ▶ Heat 3 cups of water in a saucepan. Add 2.2 lbs of sugar and stir over a low heat until the sugar has dissolved. Allow the sugar syrup to cool.

2 ◀ Peel large strips of rind from two lemons. Squeeze the juice from the fruit and discard the pith that remains. Collect 5 large elderflower heads and shake them well to remove any insects.

3 ◀ In a large glass or ceramic bowl, combine the sugar syrup, lemon juice and rind, 2 tablespoons of white wine vinegar and 7 pints of water. Add the elderflowers and stir the mixture well. Cover the bowl with a clean dish towel and let it sit for 2 days.

4 ▶ Strain the liquid and pour it into clean bottles, leaving a 2 " gap at the top. Fit corks or screw caps and store in a cool dark place for a week. If the liquid is effervescent it is ready for drinking. If bottles are to be stored, release excess gas every few days to prevent them from bursting.

Soaps & Lotions

The practice of scenting baths and applying cosmetics is hardly new, but the ingredients used have changed dramatically. Centuries ago, posies of fragrant flowers were trailed through bathwater to scent the bather and floral and herbal lotions were prepared to keep the wearer young and beautiful. These days we wash and pamper our skin with bottles of strange chemical combinations.

The making of soap is a fairly complex process but if you buy unperfumed soap you can easily add your preferred natural floral scent and remold it into shapes to suit. Baths can also be made special by hanging floral "bouquet garnis" under the running faucet.

Cosmetics, on the other hand, are easy to make at home using natural ingredients which cost far, far less than the overpackaged pots and bottles on the store shelf. Cleansing creams can be made by simmering flowers in yogurt and then whisking in a dollop of honey.

Marigolds infused in water create an ideal toner for oily skin. Beeswax and vegetable oil combine to make an effective moisturizer, which can be made fragrant with an infusion of blossoms.

Even shampoos and conditioners can be made, with recipes tailored to your own hair type. Chamomile flowers work wonders for blonde hair, marigolds for brown or red, and lavender is ideal for dark hair. These can be added to softened soap or some dried soapwort, along with an optional egg for protein, to make a healthy shampoo. Vegetable oils infused with flowers (see Project 41) are good for conditioning hair, and a small amount of melted beeswax can be added for an even richer treatment.

Without preservatives, homemade cosmetics will have a limited life, especially those based on dairy products. Make them in small quantities and store bottles in a cool place so they last as long as possible. Always label them clearly so that any friends who receive them as a gift will know what they have received and when it was made.

Most cosmetics can be made easily and cheaply using ingredients found in the cupboard or in the garden.

COSMETIC PROPERTIES

Some flowers have beneficial effects when used in creams or lotions. Here are some examples:

Chamomile (*Matricaria recutica*) - helps reduce wrinkles and tones muscles; good for delicate skin. Has a lightening effect on fair hair when used in a shampoo.

Cornflower (*Centaurea cyanus*) - eases blisters when applied in a strong infusion.

Elderflower (*Sambucus nigra*) - mildly astringent. Made into a hand cream, it will keep skin supple.

Hyssop (*Hyssopus officinalis*) - an infusion of the flowers can be applied to treat burns, bruises and insect bites.

Jasmine (*Jasminum officinale*) - makes a relaxing bath oil.

Lavender (*Lavandula vera*) - has mildly antiseptic properties which are useful in salves.

Lime flower (*Tilia europaea*) - an astringent: will stimulate the skin and help smooth wrinkles.

Marigold (*Calendula officinalis*) - strong healing properties; good for treating pimples. Makes a soothing face mask.

Mullein (*Verbascum thapsus*) - oil made from the flowers soothes diaper rash and piles.

Rose (*Rosa gallica*) - rose water is mildly astringent and hydrates the skin. Petals added to the bath will soften the skin.

Sunflower (*Helianthus annuus*) - oil from the flower heads contain vitamins B, C, E and F and is healing to the skin.

Tansy (*Tanacetum valugare*) - an infusion can be applied to treat pimples, sunburn and bruises.

Violet (*Viola odorata*) - soothes and cleanses the skin. Gently astringent; suitable for all skin types.

Wallflower (*Cheiranthus cheiri*) - soothes nerves and muscles when added to a bath.

Yarrow (*Achillea millefolium*) - cuts oiliness when used in a vinegar rinse for the hair or in skin toners.

Lavender has long been used to scent baths: its very name is derived from the Latin word meaning "to wash".

Bath bundles

Mix 1 oz dried rose petals, 1 oz dried lavender, ½ oz dried thyme and 4 oz coarse oatmeal. Cut squares of cheese-cloth and place a spoonful of the mixture in the center of each square. Gather the corners of the cloth and tie the bundle tightly with string. Tie a second knot to form a loop and hang the bundle under the hot water faucet of a bath.

PROJECT 43

Flower Cleanser

This delicate facial milk cleanser is perfect for that occasion when you want to look and feel your best. It will only keep for a few days but is a rejuvenating luxury for the skin.

1 ◀ Half fill a saucepan with water and heat until it simmers. Do not let it boil. Take the saucepan off the heat source. Pour 2 cups of fresh milk into a heat-proof bowl and place the bowl in the hot water so that the milk becomes warm.

2 ▶ Add 1 cup of flower petals to the milk. You can use any combination of violets, pansies, lavender, carnations, roses, magnolias and primulas. Stir the flowers in the milk until the water in the saucepan has cooled.

3 ▶ Blend the milk and petals until smooth. Pour the lotion into a bottle and seal. Store the bottle in a cool place and use it within a few days. After washing the face with a small amount of flower milk, rinse with cold water.

PROJECT 44

Washballs

Washballs, rounds of soap scented with flowers and herbs, were popular in the sixteenth century. A coat of petals makes them a decorative display before they are used.

1 ▶ Coarsely grate the plain white soap; you will need 2 cups of it. Crush ½ cup of dried petals (rose, lavender, jasmine or chamomile) and 2 teaspoons of dried marjoram and add to ½ cup of coarse oatmeal.

2 ▶ Measure 1 cup of rosewater and heat it until it simmers. Add the grated soap to the rosewater and stir over a gentle heat until blended. Allow to cool for ten minutes. Add a few drops of floral oil, the crushed petals and *marjoram*. Knead the mixture with your hands.

3 ◀ Roll the mixture into small balls the size of golfballs. If you wish to hang the washballs under a faucet, make a loop of ribbon and push the knot into the ball. Leave them on a sheet of wax paper for several days until they are firm.

4 ▶ Tear up extra petals into small pieces and place in a saucer. Arrange the washballs on a dish and sprinkle them with the petal fragments.

PROJECT 45

Rich Body Cream

YOU WILL NEED

red roses
olive oil
beeswax
white vinegar
cheesecloth
a glass jar
a knife & board
saucepans
a wooden spoon
a presentation jar

Here is an ancient recipe for a rich and fragrant moisturizer. It is simple to make, is based only on natural ingredients and will help to keep your skin supple.

1 ▶ Remove 4 cups of petals from fragrant red roses. If the flowers have been sprayed, wash the petals and dry them on paper towels. Chop the petals roughly and put in a jar. Cover with 4 cups of olive oil, seal and leave the jar in a warm or sunny place for a week.

2 ▶ Strain the contents of the jar through cheesecloth and discard the petals. Heat the oil in a saucepan until it is warm. Melt 1 cup of beeswax in a double saucepan over a low heat.

3 ▶ Remove both saucepans from the heat. Add the warm oil to the beeswax. Beat until the mixture is quite smooth, adding a few drops of vinegar if necessary to help them blend.

4 ◀ Beat until the mixture has cooled and is thick and smooth. Spoon it into jars and seal. Apply a little of the cream to dry skin and gently massage it in.

Sweet Flowers

Once, when sugar was not readily available as it is now, certain flowers were used as natural sweeteners. In the nineteenth century, violets were frequently added when baking. Rose petals and rosewater have been popular sweeteners since Roman times.

A practical way to capture the flavor of such flowers is to make flower sugar and add it when cooking or baking. Instructions appear on the next page. Sugar flavored with citrus blossoms is especially good with dishes based on dairy products, such as ice cream or custards. Gingerbread made with magnolia sugar is delicious, as is Jell-o flavored with lavender sugar.

The most attractive way to use flowers as sweeteners is to frost them with egg-white or crystallize them with gum arabic. Frosting is easier but the flowers are only edible for a few days. Gum arabic, a natural substance available from chemists or art supply stores, preserves flowers for several months. Instructions for both methods

appear in Projects 47 and 48.

Alternatively, you can fashion your own sweet flowers from sugarpaste. The designs in Project 46 are simple and stylized but you can make quite realistic blooms like the ones shown below. Sugarpaste, or fondant as it sometimes called, can be bought ready-made or you can use the recipe below to make your own. A word of warning: in humid weather, sugarpaste can be difficult to work and may not dry out properly.

Edible flowers can also be glazed with a toffee-like syrup to make them last longer. To make the syrup, dissolve 2 cups of sugar, 1 cup of water and ¼ teaspoon of cream of tartar in a saucepan. Stir over a low heat until a drop sets like toffee when immersed in cold water. Quickly dip the petals and lay them on a tray to set. Use glazed petals to decorate cakes or desserts.

Sugarpaste recipe
Dissolve 8 oz sugar in 3 oz water and bring to the boil. Add ½ oz liquid glucose and boil for 12 minutes. Stir with a wooden spoon and then knead until the paste is smooth.

The delicate petals of these roses are formed by pressing small balls of sugarpaste between two sheets of a plastic bag.

1 Here is one method for making flower sugar. You will need a quantity of an edible flower which has not been sprayed with insecticide: roses, violet, honeysuckle or lavender are all ideal. Remove petals to fill 2 cups, then wash and dry them. Mix with 1 cup of sugar.

2 Use a mortar and pestle to grind the petals and sugar into a fine, moist mixture. Spread the mixture on a baking tray lined with aluminium foil and dry for several hours in a very low oven. Break up the flower sugar roughly in the mortar and pestle and store it in a sealed jar in a dark place.

Delicate flowers are ideal for frosting with egg white and sugar, but take care to only choose those which are edible (see page 145) and which have not been sprayed with pesticide. These strawberry blossoms are perfectly edible.

Crystallized flowers are a charming decoration for any sweets. Instructions can be found on page 143.

PROJECT 46

Sugarpaste Circle

A pastel garland of sugarpaste flowers turns an otherwise plain cake into one fit for any celebration. Sculpting these flowers requires patience rather than expertise.

YOU WILL NEED
fondant icing
food coloring
cornflour
a sharp knife
a rolling pin & board
stiff card
a large needle
stamens
key rings
an iced cake

1 ▶ Draw each of the flower patterns onto stiff card and cut out templates. Cut off a piece of fondant icing (or see the sugarpaste recipe on page 136). Knead it until it is soft, then divide the sugarpaste into three pieces. Add food coloring to two of the pieces, kneading them again until the color is even.

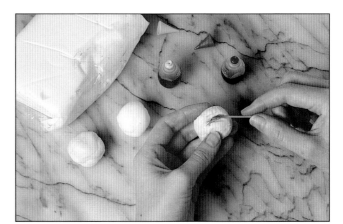

2 ▶ Dust the rolling pin and board with cornflour. Roll out each piece of sugarpaste to form a thin sheet. Lay a template on the sugarpaste and cut out flower shapes with a sharp knife.

3 ▶ Gently lay each flower in a key ring or other suitable object so that the flower is cupped. Mark a vein on each petal with the blunt end of the needle and pierce a hole in the center. Leave the flowers for several hours, until they are quite dry and stiff.

4 ▶ Cut artificial stamens (or roll tiny balls of sugarpaste). Thread several through the hole in each flower and fix them in place with a dab of moist icing at the back. When the flowers are dry once again, arrange them on an iced cake and fix them in place with icing.

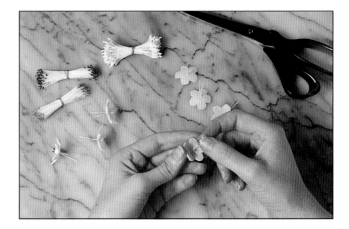

PROJECT 47

Petit Four

These dainty treats, topped with frosted flowers, are ideal for a special afternoon tea. The icing can be colored to best suit the flowers you have chosen.

YOU WILL NEED
small edible flowers
egg white
fine sugar
sponge cake
fondant icing
jam
brushes
kitchen utensils
kitchen papers
a double boiler

1 Prepare the frosted flowers a day in advance as follows. Cut the flower heads from the stems and place them on wax paper. Using a small brush, lightly coat each flower with beaten egg white.

2 Sift the fine sugar directly onto the flower heads, ensuring that all the petals are covered. The sugar that falls onto the wax paper can be resifted onto the next batch of flowers. Leave the flowers in a dry place for 24 hours.

3 Put the fondant in the top of a double boiler and melt it over boiling water. While the fondant is melting, cut the sponge into strips and then cut each strip at an angle to form diamond shapes. If necessary, slice these in half horizontally.

4 Use a brush to coat the top and sides of each sponge diamond with a light jam glaze: this will allow the icing to flow smoothly over each cake. Stir the melting fondant and, if it is still too thick, add some hot water. Add coloring and flavoring if desired.

Suggestion: Petit four can be cut in any shape. Halve squares or diamonds to make triangles. Use a cookie cutter to form round or heart-shaped pieces.

5 Use a spoon or a small ladle to drip the fondant over each cake. A small knife, dipped in boiling water, can be used to smooth out any unevenness. Decorate the petit four with the flowers before the fondant sets.

PROJECT 48

Blossom Nougat

YOU WILL NEED

edible flowers
gum arabic
flower water
fine sugar
a brush
honey
glucose
egg whites
toasted almonds
kitchen utensils

Delight a friend with a gift of delicious nougat, topped with sugared flowers. Frosted flowers can be used in place of crystallized ones, but the latter will keep longer.

1 ◀ Make sure all the flowers are dry. Dissolve 1 tablespoon of gum arabic crystals in 3 tablespoons of rosewater or orange flower water (or buy a gum arabic solution). Cut the flower heads from the stems and place them on wax paper. Using a small brush, lightly coat each flower with the gum arabic solution.

2 ▲ Sift a generous amount of fine sugar onto the flowers. Leave in a dry place for 24 hours. Turn each flower over gently and coat the backs with gum arabic and then sugar. Allow the flowers to dry completely.

3 ▲ Dissolve 1½ cups sugar and ½ cup glucose in ½ cup water. Add 4 tbsps clear honey and bring to the boil. Boil until the syrup reaches 280°F. Remove the saucepan from the heat and place it in cold water until the bubbles in the syrup subside.

4 ▶ Beat 2 egg whites until they are stiff. Roughly chop 1 cup of toasted almonds. Add the almonds and the beaten whites to the syrup and stir until it is firm.

5 ▶ Turn the nougat into a lightly greased 8 ″ square or similar sized cake pan. When the nougat is cold, cut it into squares. Top each piece with a crystallized flower. If the nougat is very sticky, wrap each square in clear cellophane.

Floral Feasts

We have all but lost the notion, enjoyed by our ancestors, of flowers as food. Now we tend to perceive flowers as purely decorative, but there was a time when flowers were cultivated alongside vegetables for their culinary value. Before imitation flavorings were available, various flowers were added to give subtle differences to bland food. Marigolds were substituted for saffron to add color and flavor to all kinds of dishes. Rosebuds were pickled in vinegar and served with cold meats and cheese. Countless other flowers were put to use in the kitchen.

Some cultures have retained the traditions of cooking with flowers. The Chinese and Japanese make liberal use of chrysanthemums. The French know the value of lavender and use it like any other herb.

With modern tastes for fresh food and healthy eating, flowers are a natural ingredient. There are many traditional recipes but experience will allow you to create your own. It is most important, however, that you eat only those flowers which you know to be edible: do not experiment if you are uncertain, as many are poisonous.

Pick flowers in the mid-morning, when they are at their most fragrant and flavorsome. If they must be washed, spray them lightly with water, shake them gently and leave them on absorbent paper. Use them as soon as possible—if you do not need them until evening, store them in a plastic bag in the refrigerator and do not pull apart flower heads until then.

Delicate petals can be sprinkled over dishes or added to sandwiches—rose petal sandwiches were considered a delicacy in the eighteenth century. Not all edible and flavorsome flowers can be eaten freshly picked—some are tough or have an odd texture. Elderflowers, zucchini flowers and others can be dipped in a light batter, fried in olive oil and served as fritters. Many flowers can be dried and then added during baking.

To draw out flavors, edible flowers can be steeped in water or brandy, or stored in oil or vinegar. These methods suit marigolds and nasturtiums, which are piquant. For naturally sweet flowers such as violets, orange blossom and primroses, storing in honey or layering in sugar are good alternatives.

Elderflowers are very good uncooked, sprinkled over salads or cold drinks.

Hibiscus flowers can be stuffed, then battered and deep-fried.

EDIBLE FLOWERS

Here are some flowers that can be eaten.
If you're not sure if a flower is edible,
check before experimenting.

Almond blossom - *Prunus dulcis*
Apple blossom - *Malus sylvestris*
Borage - *Borago officinalis*
Camellia - *Camellia japonica*
Carnation - *Dianthus caryophyllus*
Chamomile - *Matricaria recutica*
Chive flowers - *Allium schoenoprasum*
Clover - *Trifolium sp.*
Cornflower - *Centaurea cyanus*
Cowslip - *Primula veris*
Daisy - *Bellis perennis*
Dandelion - *Taraxacum officinale*
Elderflower - *Sambucus nigra*
Forget-me-not - *Myosotis alpestris*
Freesia - *Freesia x kewensis*
Fuchsia - *Fuchsia magellanica*
Gentian - *Gentiana acaulis*
Geranium - *Pelargonium graveolens*
Heartsease - *Viola tricolor*
Hibiscus - *Hibiscus sabdariffa*
Honeysuckle - *Lonicera periclymenum*
Hydrangea - *Hydrangea macrophylla*
Jasmine - *Jasminum officinale*
Lavender - *Lavandula vera*
Lime flower - *Tilia europaea*
Magnolia - *Magnolia grandiflora*
Marigold - *Calendula officinalis*
Mimosa - *Acacia dealbata*
Nasturtium - *Tropaeolum majus*
Orange blossom - *Citrus sinensis*
Pansy - *Viola tricolor*
Primrose - *Primula vulgaris*
Rose - *Rosa gallica*
Rosemary flower - *Rosmarinus officinalis*
Stock - *Matthiola incana*
Sunflower - *Helianthus annuus*
Sweet William - *Dianthus barbatus*
Thyme - *Thymus vulgaris*
Violet - *Viola odorata*
Yarrow - *Achillea millefolium*
Zinnia - *Zinnia elegans*
Zucchini flower - *Cucurbita pepo*

Nasturtiums have a tangy taste and are delicious in green salads or with tomato.

Violets and pansies can be used as a natural sweetener.

The florets from a hydrangea make edible decorations.

PROJECT 49

Petal Salad

YOU WILL NEED
olive oil
nasturtiums
salad greens
edible flowers
vinegar
a salad bowl
an airtight jar

Flowers can add color, fragrance and flavor to an otherwise ordinary salad. You can also enhance the dressing by steeping suitable flowers in oil.

1 Make the floral oil for the dressing in advance: pour 2 cups of olive oil in a jar and add 2 cups of nasturtium flowers. Seal the jar and leave it for two days, then strain the oil. Repeat the process with fresh petals until the oil is scented with the petals. Store in an airtight container.

2 Gather edible flowers early in the day. We have used dandelions, pansies, nasturtiums and zucchini flowers. See pages 144-5 for alternatives. If necessary, wash flowers and pat them dry with a paper towel. Store them in a bag in the refrigerator until needed.

3 Wash a selection of green leaves, such as lettuce, rocket, dandelion leaves, or sorrel. Shake off excess water. Tear large leaves into smaller pieces and put them in a salad bowl. Refresh flowers in cold water if necessary. Add them to the salad bowl.

4 Drizzle 4 tablespoons of floral oil over the salad and then sprinkle it with a tablespoon of vinegar. Add salt or pepper to taste. Toss the salad lightly and serve immediately. Flowers become limp and less attractive if left too long in a dressing.

PROJECT 50

Sugar Cookies

These tokens of affection can be made in different shapes to suit the occasion. They are made with carnation sugar which adds a subtle flavor and hue.

YOU WILL NEED
edible flower petals
sugar
butter
plain flour
an egg
a mortar & pestle
rolling pin & board
a cookie cutter
a baking tray
a spatula

1 ▶ *Flavor sugar with flower petals (see page 137 for instructions on making flower sugar). You will need less than 1 cup for this recipe. The petals of clove carnations (also known as clove pinks) add a delicate clove flavor.*

2 ▶ *Sift 2 cups plain flour into a large bowl. Rub ¾ cup butter into the flour with your fingers. Add ½ cup flower sugar and a lightly beaten egg and mix all the ingredients to form a ball.*

3 ◀ *Roll the mixture out on a board until it is quite thin. Cut out shapes with a cookie cutter or a sharp knife and place them on a lightly greased tray.*

4 ▶ *Bake the cookies in a moderate oven (350°F) until they start to turn a golden color (approximately 15 minutes. Remove from the oven and sprinkle with extra flower sugar while they are still hot.*

Suggestion: To make cookies which can be hung as decorations, pierce a hole before baking and thread with a narrow ribbon when the cookies are cool.

PROJECT 51

Rose Petal Jam

YOU WILL NEED
fragrant red roses
sugar
lemon juice
rosewater
a large saucepan
jam jars
fabric covers
ribbon
labels

What better gift to offer friends and family than homemade rose petal jam? If properly sealed, the conserve should keep for many months and is delicious on scones and teacakes.

1 Remove petals from 20 fragrant red roses. Pinch out the bitter white part at the base of each petal. Measure 5 cups of petals and rinse them with cold water.

2 Place the petals and 2½ cups of water in a steel saucepan and bring to the boil. Cover and simmer for 30 minutes. Strain the petals from the liquid and reserve both.

3 Return the liquid to the saucepan and add 1½ cups sugar, 1 tablespoon rosewater and 2 tablespoons lemon juice. Stir over a low heat until the sugar dissolves. Boil, without stirring, for at least 10 minutes.

4 Test whether the jam has set by dropping a little hot jam onto a cold plate: if a skin forms as it cools the jam is set. When the jam is set, stir in the cooked petals which have been reserved.

5 Pour the jam into clean, warm jars. When the jam has cooled, seal the jars. Write a label and decorate with a round of fabric and a matching ribbon. Store in a cool, dark place.

Gift Giving

In these days of mass production and mass consumption the art of giving is sadly endangered. Flowers are one of the few things that give a clear uncluttered message of love and gratitude. A handmade gift is another, and the combination of flowers and something you have made yourself conveys the most potent message of all.

This book contains many ideas for gifts crafted from flowers. Page 155 lists just a few possibilities for matching projects to events. For an extra special occasion or for someone who is particularly important to you, consider preparing a basket of some smaller items. Some friends will no doubt have floral favorites. Make a note of any you discover and show your thoughtfulness by presenting them with their preferred flowers. Alternatively, you can rely on the "language of flowers". By tradition, many flowers have specific meanings attributed to them. The rose, of course, symbolizes love. White bellflowers imply gratitude, tulips indicate fame. A posy of flowers is extremely eloquent, although you might have to make more obscure messages clear with a few words! Suggestions for wrapping gifts of arranged flowers are given on pages 156-157.

Even if you are giving something other than flowers, a simple floral spray on the wrapped or boxed present will make it even more special. Pressed flowers arranged on a greeting card are an ideal way to send flowers through the post. See Project 29 and pages 158-159 for some attractive ideas.

No matter what form a floral gift takes, you can be sure it will be enjoyed, possibly even as much as you enjoyed making it.

Add a miniature bouquet to your wrapped or boxed present.

Beautiful boxes

Plain boxes can be turned into something special with some ribbon and a few dried flowers. Choose twisted paper ribbon in a color to complement your flowers, unravel a length and stretch it over the box lid. Cut and glue the ends on the inside rim. Repeat this for the box base so that it matches the lid. Arrange dried leaves in the center of the lid and glue them in place using a glue gun. Glue on dried flowers (we have used white roses), taking care to conceal any stems. The box can be opened without removing the ribbon or disturbing the arrangement.

Perfect packaging

Rose petals make a lovely lining for a delicate gift. Use dried petals if the present must be sent over a long distance.

Celebrating with Flowers

Flowers have always played a major role in the festivities we enjoy each year. Floral displays celebrate the season of spring and the rebirth that Easter implies. Garlands of flowers are traditionally worn to mark mid-summer. Harvest festivals and Thanksgiving dinners are incomplete without arrangements of grasses, fruit and flowers. The Christmas period is marked with swags of holly and other evergreens. All these celebrations confirm our links to the natural world and the inclusion of flowers as an integral part of them is only fitting.

Milestones in our lives are also marked with flowers. Many people would consider a wedding incomplete without bridal bouquets, corsages and elaborate arrangements. Births, coming-of-age celebrations and even deaths are all marked with flowers, making each event more poignant and memorable.

Some occasions offer too good an excuse to miss. The gift of flowers on Valentine's Day is a natural way of signaling your affection for someone. Parents also deserve a floral tribute regularly and both Mother's and Father's Days provide ideal opportunities for showing your appreciation. Those major wedding anniversaries—silver for 25 years, golden for 50—are worthy of a grand arrangement, created with silvery-white and golden flowers respectively.

Friends can be remembered on birthdays and also at times when they are unwell or a little disheartened. Perfumed flowers go a long way towards lifting the spirits.

No matter what the occasion, flowers, or a gift crafted from flowers, will be very fitting. On the next page are suggestions for just some of the projects in this book which can be given at those special times.

Confetti
A shower of fresh petals is so much nicer than paper confetti. Store the petals in a plastic bag in the refrigerator until they are needed.

Baby Shower
Petal Welcome (Project 5)
Spring Border (Project 13)
Potpourri Sachets (Project 23)
Daffodils (Project 25)
Petal Frame (Project 35)

Christmas
Christmas Swag (Project 12)
Christmas Mix (Project 24)
Festive Card (Project 29)
Gilt Decorations (Project 31)
Felt Poinsettia (Project 37)

Valentine
Perfect Posy (Project 2)
Rosebud Ball (Project 10)
Valentine Garland (Project 20)
Flower Cleanser (Project 43)
Sugar Cookies (Project 50)

Thanksgiving
Potted Garden (Project 4)
Vinegar Basket (Project 18)
Door Wreath (Project 21)
Citrus Room Scent (Project 22)
Rose Petal Jam (Project 51)

Wedding shower
Candle Rings (Project 7)
Petal Frame (Project 14)
Potpourri Sachets (Project 23)
Porcelain Roses (Project 33)
Elderflower Fizz (Project 42)

Get Well
Country Stack (Project 5)
Cornflower Spray (Project 35)
Lavender Bottles (Project 25)
Bath Oil (Project 41)
Blossom Nougat (Project 48)

Housewarming
Raffia Plait (Project 11)
Door Wreath (Project 21)
Pressed Sampler (Project 28)
Lining Paper (Project 26)
Jasmine Tea (Project 40)
Washballs (Project 44)
Rose Petal Jam (Project 51)

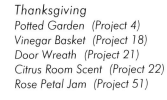

Wrapping Flowers

A gift of flowers, like any other gift, needs to be wrapped to be complete. The aim is not to conceal the nature of the present but simply to add the finishing touch which will show how much care has been taken.

These days, there are many lovely commercial giftwraps available. Waterproof wrappings are essential if you wish to soak the stems of a posy or bouquet. Clear cellophane allows the beauty of the flowers to show through and can be decorated with a colorful bow. Foil, often used by florists, is also waterproof. Other wrappings, such as tissue paper, are suitable for dried flowers or for fresh ones with dry stems.

If you want to use a patterned paper, choose one that complements the colors of the flowers. Alternatively, you might consider using plain brown paper tied with a raffia bow for a more natural effect.

Show your thoughtfulness in the presentation: a bowl of flowers is ideal for a disabled or elderly person who may have difficulty rearranging a bouquet. A fitting housewarming gift might include both flowers and an attractive container.

Gifts of flowers that must be kept upright, such as potted plants or displays in a bowl, can be safely wrapped in a pyramid box, as shown on the next page.

1 ▶ *To wrap a posy and keep it moist for traveling, cup several paper tissues around the stems. Spray with water until quite damp.*

2 ▶ *Fold a cellophane sheet at an angle and wrap it around the posy. Repeat with another sheet. Form a bow from wired ribbon and thread an extra piece of ribbon through the back of it. Tie this tightly around the cellophane-wrapped stems and arrange the bow.*

To wrap a potted plant as a gift, lay two squares of paper or cellophane, one square and the other at an angle. Place the pot in the center and bring the corners of the paper up around it, securing it around the pot with an elastic band. Cover this with a ribbon and bow and flare the corners of the wrapping.

Here is one way to wrap a standing arrangement or a pot plant. Measure and cut a card triangle with sides more than twice the height of the flower display. Score a triangle in the center, as per the dotted lines in the diagram, and fold up the sides around the flowers. Punch a hole in each corner, thread a ribbon through and tie it in a bow.

Making Tags & Cards

A greeting card is a way of telling someone that you are thinking of them. What better way to say it than with a few flowers? A flower press stocked with a selection of flowers, some glue and a few pieces of card or stiff paper are all you need to create personalized and beautiful cards or gift tags.

Most greeting cards are single folds with a design on the front. To frame a design in a card, use a three-panel mount such as the one on the bottom right of page 159. Blank mounts can be bought in craft stores or you can make your own by folding a piece of card into three panels and cutting a window in the center panel.

As greeting cards are often given or sent in envelopes, an arrangement of pressed flowers is the best way to decorate them. Gift tags, on the other hand, do not need to be perfectly flat and can be adorned with small dried flowers. Tags can be cut in any shape to suit the occasion.

Cards, envelopes and wrapping paper can all be scented by storing them for a while with a potpourri. Make a number of cards at the one time so you have a ready supply.

Tag ribbons
Fold a length of ribbon in half and pull the folded end part way through a hole in the tag to form a loop. Thread the two ends through the loop and pull tight.

Tag shapes
A favorite shape for a gift tag is the old parcel tag shape: a rectangle with two corners clipped. Tags can be any shape, as long as there is room for the message!

Top left: A garland of pressed and sprayed flowers
Above: A miniature spray of dried flowers
Below: Pressed flowers in a three-panel mount
Left: A pretty bouquet of pressed flowers

Index